Comanche Midnight

Comanche Midnight

Essays by Stephen Harrigan

University of Texas Press
Austin

Requests for permission to reproduce material from this work should be sent to Permissions, University of Texas Press, Box 7819, Austin, TX 78713-7819.

(∞) The paper used in this publication meets the minimum requirements of American National Standard for Information Sciences—Permanence of Paper for Printed Library Materials, ANSI Z39.48-1984.

Cataloging-in-Publication Information

Harrigan, Stephen, 1948–
    Comanche midnight / Stephen Harrigan — 1st ed.
        p.   cm.
    ISBN 0-292-73088-8 (cloth : alk. paper). —
    ISBN 0-292-73096-9 (paper : alk. paper)
    I. Title.
PS3558.A626C66   1995
814'.54dc20   94-23983

"Comanche Midnight" originally published as "The Lost Tribe," reprinted with permission from the February 1989 issue of TEXAS MONTHLY. "The Temple of Destiny" reprinted with permission from the July 1989 issue of TEXAS MONTHLY. "The Soul of Treaty Oak," originally published as "Vigil at Treaty Oak," reprinted with permission from the October 1989 issue of TEXAS MONTHLY. "Highway One" reprinted with permission from the January 1991 issue of TEXAS MONTHLY. "The Bay," originally published as "Worked to Death," reprinted with permission from the October 1988 issue of TEXAS MONTHLY. "Taking Care of Lonesome Dove," originally published as "The Making of Lonesome Dove," reprinted with permission from the June 1988 issue of TEXAS MONTHLY. "Feeling Flush" originally appeared as "Monte Carlo" in the February 1993 issue of Travel Holiday. "The Anger of Achilles," originally published as "The Eye of the Beholder," reprinted with permission from the October 1986 issue of TEXAS MONTHLY. "Eighteen Minutes" reprinted with permission from the April 1986 issue of TEXAS MONTHLY. "Rock and Sky" originally appeared as "Anasazi Country" in the July/August 1991 issue of Travel Holiday. "The Tiger Is God," originally published as "Nature of the Beast," reprinted with permission from the July 1988 issue of TEXAS MONTHLY. "Selling the Ranch," originally published as "Wild Forever," reprinted with permission from the December 1989 issue of TEXAS MONTHLY. "Swamp Thing" reprinted with permission from the January 1990 issue of TEXAS MONTHLY. "The Roof of Eden" originally appeared as "Rocky Mountain National Park" in the February 1990 issue of Travel Holiday. "The Man Nobody Knows" originally appeared as "The Long Lost Hunter" in the September/October 1992 issue of Audubon.

For Jim,

Julie, and Tom

Contents

Author's Note

When I was writing the pieces in this book, I never thought to refer to them as essays. As a staff writer for *Texas Monthly*, and later as a freelance journalist, I was immersed in the nomenclature of the magazine world, which has no loftier term for a piece of writing than article or story. Essays, to my johnny-deadline mind, were produced in rustic New England cottages by cultured observers with all the time in the world to ponder how the beating of a moth's wings on a window pane mirrors the eternal strivings of the human soul. In contrast, my own efforts were written always against a ticking clock, often in the teeth of financial catastrophe, and with a philosophical sangfroid when it came to the inevitable bartering for space with the art department, or the wrangling with ever-vigilant copy editors and fact checkers over exactly which words I would be allowed to use. I felt lucky and proud that I was able to make a living as a writer. I admired the quick and unpretentious minds of my colleagues, and I enjoyed the challenge of shepherding my prose through the often grinding realities of the publishing process. But I'm not sure I ever really got the hang of writing articles. Reporting came harder to me than musing, and facts never registered in my mind with anywhere near the staying power of feelings. Nevertheless, I felt I had something urgent to say, and the real-life demands of journalism helped train my mind away from the aimless introspection to which it is naturally prone.

But magazine articles, by and large, are short-lived phenomena. There was nothing more demoralizing to me than to come across my work years after its shelf life had expired, tucked in among advertisements for products that had once been fashionable, headlines and captions that had once been bitingly clever, and yellowed pages that had once been so glossy they hurt your eyes. Writing as the deadlines approached, I was always deadly conscious that, as much as I was able, I must build my articles to last. I wanted them safely protected within the covers of a book. Books are not timeless either, of course, as the rows of musty, unwanted titles in used bookstores attest, but they do provide a far better illusion of immortality than magazines.

In assembling a book like this one, there is a natural tendency for the writer to think of it hopefully as more than the sum of its parts, as a solid coherent statement rather than a scattershot collection. I've tried not to saddle *Comanche Midnight* with aspirations it cannot fulfill, but on the other hand I don't believe that the components of this book came together by accident. For every piece I've included, there are two or three others that are still mouldering in the lost-magazine graveyard. Some of them don't deserve to be resurrected, and in fact it would pain me to think anybody would ever read them again. Others, though, are pretty good. I left them out because, in some vague way, they didn't belong. There is no great theme to this book that I can decipher, but it seems to me that all the pieces at least share the same frequency. They address my old preoccupations with worlds that have vanished, communication that is sealed off, perceptions that are out of reach. There is an air of mystery about them, and it is that mystery that finally emboldens me to think of them as true essays. They are a record not just of certain events and people and places, but of the mind that witnessed them, and that is still trying to grasp what it beheld.

Acknowledgments

A journalist's great overriding debt is always to his subjects, and I would like to thank the people who appear in this book for sharing with me their time and trust. I am grateful as well to the staffs of *Texas Monthly*, *Travel Holiday*, and *Audubon*, in whose pages these essays first appeared. My editors at those magazines—Gregory Curtis, Maggie Staats Simmons, and Linda Perney—provided me not just with reporting opportunities but with the insight and conviction that allowed me to make the most of them. I was also dependent on the help, expertise, or encouragement of Michael Levy, Paul Burka, Patricia Sharpe, Catherine Flato, Charles Simmons,

Michael Robbins, Elizabeth Crook, and Lawrence Wright. My most recent debt, and among the happiest to acknowledge, is to the staff of the University of Texas Press. Then there are my wife Sue Ellen and our three daughters, to whom my gratitude is bound up with love and homage.

Comanche Midnight

Comanche Midnight

Marie was seven years old today, and the sweat was for her. She arrived at the sweat lodge clutching a baby doll and a bottle of Mountain Dew. Gayle Niyah-Hughes, her mother, had brought along a Care Bear birthday cake for afterward and some prayer ties that she had made herself.

"There's one for me and one for her," she explained, fingering the little pouches filled with tobacco and sweet grass that would be burned in the fire pit so that the smoke would rise like a tangible prayer. "I don't make the best ones, but it probably doesn't matter if they're not perfect. I just wanted to have this for my daughter. It'll mean more to her than having a party at Pizza Hut."

Seven men had gathered to do the sweat and pray for Marie. One of them—judging from the sharpness of his features and the moustache that grew only in two small tufts at the sides of his mouth—was close to being a full-blood Apache. Most of the others were, in varying degrees of heritage, the people I had come to Oklahoma to find: Comanches.

Like many other modern Texans—heirs to the conquest—I could not help regarding Comanches with a romantic cast of mind, as some long-ago blood enemy, as the personification of the frontier itself. The Comanches once dominated much of Texas from the Edwards Plateau to the High Plains. Though in the end they lost it all, the intensity of their defiance is commemorated in the pitiless and self-reliant Texan character.

In my imagination the Comanches belonged to history, and it was easy to think of them as extinct. They were an emblem of barbaric splendor, and as such it was tempting to believe they had not been subdued but had merely vanished like a prairie wind. But the Comanches did not vanish. They are still around, though much of their culture has long since been destroyed or mislaid. They are a people haunted by the richness and vigor of their past, haunted all the more as each new generation devolves farther away—in language, in blood, in logic—from the ancestral ideal. In that sense, they are like everyone else on earth: a people struggling to recall who they were and to understand who they have become.

When the sun was a little lower, Kenneth Coosewoon, the sweat leader, began taking his ceremonial instruments out of a lacquered-wood carrying case the size of a small toolbox. There were bundles of braided sweet grass, an eagle feather, a gourd, and a deerskin pouch containing sticks of wood that he had found glowing one night on a creek bank. Coosewoon wore a black jogging suit and glasses. His grayish hair was long and tied back, and a beaded medicine bundle hung around his neck.

In the old days the sweat lodge was an important fixture in a Comanche camp. It was a center for prayer and purification. Before a young man undertook a vision quest or a group of warriors embarked on a raid they would prepare themselves spiritually in the sweat lodge. No one knew any longer exactly what the Comanche sweat ritual had been, so Coosewoon more or less had to improvise. Like many other facets of contemporary Comanche culture, the sweat ceremony was a pastiche of half-remembered lore, gleanings from other tribes, and bits and pieces of Christian dogma.

"I never even dreamed I'd run a sweat," Coosewoon told me as he gathered his things together. He was the director of the alcoholism center in Lawton, and several years ago he had gotten interested in the sweat ritual as a kind of therapeutic extension of the Alcoholics Anonymous program. He advertised in the paper for someone who knew the old ways and could run a sweat, but no one answered the ad. Then one day he was praying at the creek bank when he saw the glowing wood. The wood was hot to the touch, and at the moment he picked it up he heard a bird shriek and a big oak tree shake in the wind, and then a spirit spoke to him.

"The spirit said, 'You don't need nobody. You go ahead and run the sweat. Just be yourself. I'll be with you all the time to help you.'

"He said everything would come to me and everything has come to me. I was given stuff little by little. An eagle feather. A gourd. I was given a pipe, but I ain't never fired it up yet. A Sioux medicine man named Black Elk told me to pray with it and respect it and it will tell me when it's all right to fire it up. In the old days we would have had a pipe carrier to work with me on it, but we don't have any of those guys anymore."

The sweat lodge was made of heavy canvas draped over a cured willow frame. It was a low, hemispherical structure whose entrance faced east, the source of wisdom and knowledge. When it was nearly dusk we stripped down to gym shorts or bathing suits and crawled inside. There was a deep pit in the center, and the bare earth surrounding the pit was covered with strips of old carpet. Dried sage hung from the bent willow poles, and Gayle fixed the medicine ties for her and Marie onto the frame above their heads. One by one, seven heated rocks from a bonfire outside were brought into the lodge on two forked branches and lowered into the pit. Coosewoon blessed the glowing stones, brushing them with the braided sweet grass, and then sprinkled cedar over the pit, filling the lodge with its harsh and aromatic smell.

"Grandfather," he prayed, "thank you for the lives of the people in this lodge. Thank you for the earth and for our Indian people, Grandfather. And we ask your help for all the Indians who are stumbling around drunk, Grandfather, who are not walking straight on Mother Earth, Grandfather. And we thank you especially for the life of Marie, Grandfather, and we pray that you show her how to walk firmly on the earth, Grandfather, and show her how to travel the four directions . . ."

When Coosewoon was finished, he said, "Ahoh! All my relations!" and then each person in the lodge prayed in turn. Just when the dry heat from the rocks began to be uncomfortable, Coosewoon doused them with water, and we began to steep in the purging humid air. The others' prayers were direct and unaffected pleas for deliverance—from alcoholism, from broken hopes, from the diabetes that kept loved ones in the Indian hospital, waiting for their legs to be amputated.

"Heavenly father," Gayle said when it was her turn, "I thank you for the life of Marie. When I first saw her seven years ago, Lord, I was *scared* because I know life is so hard, Lord. Lord, I thank you for the life of my husband, even though he's been gone for three years. I know it's wrong to grieve over his death, that I should be thankful for what I have, but it's so *hard*, Lord. Lord, I ask you to bless me and Marie and my children that are still unborn. Help me to understand the ways of our Indian people. Ahoh! All my relations!"

The sweat took place in four stages, with the participants leaving the lodge every half hour or so to replenish themselves in the cool night air. After each break more stones were brought in, and before the water was poured over them they glowed in the pit, the only light in the utter darkness of the lodge. During the second session Coosewoon sang a song that had been given to him by an old woman a few years before, accompanying himself by shaking a gourd.

"Hey! ya-ya-ya-ya—Hoh! nya-no-nya-no," or so the song sounded to me, its primitive rhythm oddly complex and familiar.

The steam made me lightheaded and short of breath. And in that dark lodge, filled with ancient music and the smell of sage and cedar, I found myself entertaining the illusion that the last two hundred years of history had never taken place, that the Comanches were still and always would be the lords of the plains.

In the old days the Comanches knew themselves as Nermernuh, a term that—like so many other self-designations of American Indians—has one simple, confident meaning: "People." In the sign language used by the Plains tribes, the Nermernuh were represented by a wiggling motion of the hand that symbolized a snake traveling backward. The Utes—their historic enemies—knew the Nermernuh as Koh-mahts, "Those who are always against us," and it was a corrupted version of that name that finally prevailed among outsiders.

At the height of their power the Comanches presided over a vast swath of prairie, desert, and mountain foothills that became known as Comancheria. They roamed as far north as Nebraska, and their raids carried them as far east as the Gulf Coast and deep enough into Mexico to encounter rain forests and to come home bearing legends of "little hairy men with tails."

The Comanches were stocky, barrel-chested, prone to nearsightedness. Their faces were broad, with heavy, looming features. The men were vain and superstitious about their hair, keeping it long and greased with buffalo dung, and their ceremonial leggings and moccasins were distinguished by long trails of fringe that dragged on the ground. Comanches filled the cavities in their teeth with dried mushrooms, powdered their babies with cotton-wood rot, and directed attention to their war wounds by outlining the scars with tattoos. Boys shot humming-birds out of the air, snaring them in the split shaft of an arrow. Although there was no prescribed cosmology, the Comanches had a complex and appreciative awareness of a world brimming with spirits and half-glimpsed designs. Unlike other Plains tribes, they did not have an overarching tribal unity. The Comanches were parceled out into bands and each band was an ad hoc government unto itself, led by men who had become chiefs not through any formal process but through the uncontested power of their personalities.

Long before, when they first filtered down out of the

eastern Rockies onto the plains, the Comanches had been just another wandering tribe of bandy-legged pedestrians. But when they encountered the shaggy mustangs that the Spanish had brought to the New World, it was as if they had found some long-missing component of their own identity. The Comanches adapted to the horse with breathtaking commitment. They understood better than any other Indians what a powerful new technology this creature represented. The Apaches, for instance, made only limited use of the horse as a war tool, using it to carry them longer distances on a raid but ultimately dismounting to fight. Comanches fought on horseback, seated on rawhide facsimiles of Spanish saddles or hanging low along the horse's shoulder, loosing arrows from beneath its neck.

They learned to breed horses and became wealthy by plains standards. It was not unusual for a Comanche warrior to have a string of 250 ponies, for a chief to have as many as 1,500.

The horse made the Comanches dangerous, but they had always been predators. Boys became men, and men acquired status, primarily through deeds of war. Texas history is filled with accounts—some bogus, some not—of Comanche savagery. Settlers who encountered the mutilated bodies of their loved ones—the scalps taken, the genitals ripped off, the entrails baking in the sun—were understandably eager to propagate the notion that Comanches were demons who wallowed in the blackest depths of human cruelty. Torture and ritual mutilation were not confined to the Indians, of course. The difference was that white society had learned to fear and scorn in itself the very bloodlust that the Comanches openly celebrated.

For hundreds of years the Comanches held the plains by right of conquest. They were able to keep Spain from establishing an effective colonial claim on Texas, and they fought the more relentless American juggernaut with desperate ferocity through many bitter generations. But by 1874—the year of the pivotal battle at Adobe Walls—it was pretty much over. Most of the bands— their populations halved by disease, their livelihood and morale shattered by the unimaginable efficiency with which the hide hunters were destroying the buffalo—had already retreated along with the Kiowas and Apaches to the reservation at Fort Sill in southwest Oklahoma. Seven years earlier, at the Treaty of Medicine Lodge, a Comanche chief named Ten Bears—who had visited Abraham Lincoln in the White House and had been shown Comancheria on a great globe in the State Department—had made a speech of defiance that was in tone an unmistakable elegy: "I was born upon the prairie, where the wind blew free and there was nothing to break the light of the sun. I was born where there were no enclosures and everything drew a free breath. . . . If the Texans had kept out of my country, there might have been peace. . . . But it is too late. The whites have the country which we loved, and we wish only to wander on the prairie until we die . . ."

The Comanches knew they were living in an apocalyptic time, and they were susceptible to any sort of messianic logic that could fuel their resistance. A young man called Ishatai—whose name translated to "Coyote Drippings"—rose up among them as a prophet. He was credited with predicting the appearance of a comet, claimed miraculous powers, and asserted with conviction what the Comanches most longed to hear: that the white men could be driven from the plains, that the buffalo could be restored, that life as it had always been understood could resume. Ishatai inspired an avenging alliance of Comanches, Kiowas, and Cheyennes. The first objective was Adobe Walls, an isolated trading post a few miles north of the Canadian River in the Texas Panhandle that had been set up to accommodate the hide hunters and skinners who had come south to annihilate the last great herds of buffalo.

Though Ishatai was a spiritual leader, he did not claim to be a war chief. That role, according to legend, fell to Quanah, a prominent young warrior from the Kwahadi band who was destined to become the most famous Comanche who ever lived. Quanah was the son of a chief named Peta Nocona and the celebrated white captive Cynthia Ann Parker. Cynthia Ann had been seized by the Comanches at the age of nine on a terror-filled day in 1836 when the Indians had raided her family's settlement in East Texas. Her adjustment to Comanche ways was thorough—she married Peta Nocona and bore him three children, including Quanah—but her life was bracketed by shock and heartbreak. After twenty-five years as a Comanche she was recaptured when Texas Rangers raided a camp on the Pease River. Though Cynthia Ann could speak no English, she broke into confused tears when she heard her name. She and her fifteen-month-old daughter, Topsannah, were treated with kindness, and the Texas Legislature even voted her a pension. But her one wish—to be released back onto the prairie with the rest of her family—was denied. When her daughter died she grieved with the savage intensity of a Comanche mother, and not long after that she herself perished from what has variously been described as a broken heart, a "strange fever," or self-starvation.

Quanah was a teenager when his mother was stolen from his world. At the time of the battle of Adobe Walls he was about twenty—a cunning, fearless, embittered warrior commanding a force of perhaps seven hundred men, who, thanks to Ishatai's mystical power—his medicine—believed themselves magically invincible. The Indians arrived at Adobe Walls on a warm June night and attacked the collection of sod buildings in the predawn darkness of the next morning. Adobe Walls was inhabited that night by fewer than thirty buffalo hunters and storekeepers, and Quanah had counted on overrunning them while they slept. But the buffalo men had been up most of the night fixing a broken roof support in the saloon, and their wakefulness spoiled the surprise attack. The defenders managed to barricade themselves in time, though one man was killed as he ran for cover, and two brothers, German teamsters who had been sleeping in their wagon, were discovered and brutally dispatched. The frustrated Indians even scalped the teamsters' dog.

The raid quickly turned into a disaster. The Indians—whose notion of warfare relied on individual initiative and abrupt, feinting charges—were unprepared for a coordinated assault on an entrenched position. The hide hunters, on the other hand, were superb marksmen, accustomed to leisurely potting hundreds of buffalo a day at long range with their Sharps rifles. As warrior after warrior went down, the Comanches and their allies quickly discovered that Ishatai's protective medicine was a cruel illusion. Quanah himself was wounded. Three quarters of a mile away, at the top of a low mesa, wearing nothing but his yellow medicine paint, the prophet Ishatai sat on his horse, watching the fight. His powers had proven so ineffective that they could not even protect a warrior next to him who was knocked from his horse by a spectacular shot from one of the distant buffalo guns.

After a lingering siege that lasted three days, the attackers withdrew, unable to recover their dead. The buffalo hunters cut off the heads of the Indians they had killed and impaled them on stakes. The alliance that Ishatai had put together fell apart, and though Quanah and his band continued raiding for some months afterward, the medicine was gone. That fall, U.S. soldiers surprised a Kwahadi camp in Palo Duro Canyon and captured most of the remaining free Comanches. Then they shot the Indians' horses. Nine months later Quanah and Ishatai led the People, under army escort, onto the reservation. The trek to Fort Sill took a month. A doctor who accompanied the Comanches and joined them on their last buffalo hunt as free men had the time of his life. "I never feel so delighted," he wrote, unwittingly memorializing the vanished joys of Comanche existence, "as when mounted on a fleet horse bounding over the prairie."

"We must have been an ornery group of people," Kenneth Saupitty, the chairman of the Comanche Tribal Business Committee, reflected as we sat one October morning in his office. Saupitty was, in effect, the Comanche chief, though that title had been retired after Quanah's death. ("Resting here until day breaks and shadows fall and darkness disappears," reads his tombstone in the Fort Sill post cemetery. "Quanah Parker, Last Chief of the Comanches.") Saupitty was fifty-one but looked younger. His hair was short, with no gray in it, and his cordial, chatty demeanor made him seem at first acquaintance more like a middle manager than the chief executive of an Indian nation.

The chairman's office is located in a wing of the

Comanche Tribal Complex, which sits on a rise just off the H. E. Bailey Turnpike, a few miles north of Lawton. The building has the anonymous multipurpose design of a nursing home or a municipal annex. The day I was there, a Ford Aerostar was parked on the lawn, next to a monument that listed the names of Comanche warriors from Adobe Walls to Vietnam. The Aerostar was a bingo prize that was to be given away the next weekend in a game of Bonanza.

There are eight thousand four hundred and ten Comanches. About half of them still live here around the old reservation lands of southwest Oklahoma. To officially be a Comanche, to be counted on the tribal rolls, a person must have a "blood quantum" of at least one fourth. Once enrolled, a member is eligible to vote for the officers of the Tribal Business Committee and to qualify for the various assistance programs and grants that are channeled to Native Americans through the Bureau of Indian Affairs.

Comanches no longer have a reservation. It ceased to exist in 1901, the year the federal government implemented the Jerome Agreement, a scheme by which the reservation was broken up for the benefit of white entrepreneurs and settlers who had long coveted the Indian land. In compensation, each Indian was given an allotment of 160 acres in the hope that this would force the Comanches to become assimilated homesteaders rather than wards of the government. To a small degree, it worked. Most Comanches didn't become farmers of their own allotted lands but leased them out instead. For a time, the lease payments provided a reliable economic base, though with each new wave of descendants the per capita value of the original parcels grew more and more diluted. Of greater importance was the fact that allotment, which brought with it a flood of settlement into Indian country, put jobs for the first time within practical reach of most Comanches.

But whatever prosperity has come to the Comanches has been decidedly marginal. Comanches have all the familiar problems of other Indian peoples, including staggering rates of alcoholism and diabetes. And for all the worldly benefits that came with allotment, nearly half of the Comanches in the Lawton area are unemployed. Those who have jobs—who are fortunate enough to be employed as civilian workers at Fort Sill or as bureaucrats at the Tribal Complex or the BIA—often have extensive kinship obligations that leave them supporting as many as a dozen people on one salary.

The Comanches may have lost their reservation, but there do still seem to reside within them the traces of a reservation mentality. Though they never became tillers of the soil as the whites expected them to, they did cease to be nomads. They clung to the old reservation the way their ancestors might have lingered at a dying campfire. The Second World War, in which many Comanches served, helped to disperse them somewhat, but few of the People became wholeheartedly cosmopolitan enough to take on the alien priorities of the white man's world.

As I visited Comanches I kept sensing a kind of languor, a reliance on certain earthly rhythms that white people do not seem to feel. Many of them were poor, and though they were certainly not poor by choice it seemed to me that as a people they shared a fundamental disinterest in the ideal of wealth. Even the dynamic rhetoric I encountered at the level of tribal government had the air of mimicry.

"I have maintained," Saupitty was telling me, "that we don't have a choice as far as economic development goes. We've got to provide work in some way. We've got a big bingo expansion coming up. We're moving it into downtown Lawton, right off the interstate access. We're talking a fifteen-thousand seater. Then we're going to expand the complex. At this point we're thinking about an amphitheater, maybe a KOA campground, a store that would be an outlet for souvenirs. We've looked at horse racing. Horses and Comanches should be compatible.

"Horses and Comanches," he mused. "You know, we've been told about that by books and movies all our lives." He looked up at a woman who was passing out agendas. "What about you, Joyce, can you ride a horse?"

"I was thrown off once," she said. "Haven't been back on since."

The old Comanche way of life came to an end with such punishing swiftness that, to an outsider, the Comanches of today still seem to be trying to absorb the shock. At one moment the People were running after wild buffalo on the plains, wolfing down the animals' raw livers and gall bladders, and then, in the wink of an eye, there they were on the reservation, wearing shoddy preacher clothes and gouging Mother Earth with plows. If there was ever a group of people not meant to be farmers, it was the Comanches. On the reservation they sometimes chased after cattle on horseback, filling them full of arrows and bullets and then cutting them open and feeding the steaming offal to their children.

Some Comanches, of course, were more flexible than others. Quanah—now Quanah Parker—became a spectacular success in this strange new world and before long was one of the most celebrated and richest Indians in the country. His half-white blood, his regal bearing, and his status as a revered former enemy made him a sentimental favorite among his conquerors. A group of ranchers built him a 32-room house whose roof was painted with giant white stars. He invested $40,000 in a railroad, the Quanah, Acme, and Pacific. He had his own stationery, a per diem for official travel, and even a place in Theodore Roosevelt's inaugural parade.

In other ways Quanah hewed to his former life. He had numerous wives, and when he was instructed by the reservation agent to get rid of all but one he responded by saying that was fine with him, as long as the agent was the one who broke the news to the disenfranchised wives. He had no interest in the teachings of the missionaries— Baptist, Mennonite, Catholic, Dutch Reformed—who descended upon the reservation and instead turned to the "pagan" peyote religion that was becoming increasingly important to the demoralized Indian peoples of the Southwest. Quanah initially opposed the allotment program, but he was still regarded by many of his people as a sellout, and they remembered that it was the white men who had appointed him chief of the Comanches.

Comanches are individuals, and Comanche politics is therefore contentious and confused. I was never certain, as I listened to accounts of recent tribal history, exactly which chairman had been recalled when, which members of the business committee had used tribal funds to lease Learjets and start fast-food franchises, which officials stood accused of outright embezzlement. Saupitty himself was recalled—illegally, he maintains—during his first term, in 1980. In reaction, a group of his supporters seized the complex, charging the originators of the recall with misappropriation of funds and demanding an audit. The standoff lasted six months. Some Comanches applauded the activists and camped out in their tepees in support; others threatened an armed assault. The crisis finally dissolved, but not before the Bureau of Indian Affairs suspended all federal funds until the Comanches resolved their differences. Today the affair—the Comanche Civil War—is commemorated by a small plaque that sits in a stubbly field next to the complex. To read the inscription, one has to crawl through a barbed-wire fence.

Long ago, when the Comanches wandered unimpeded across the plains, they would occasionally happen upon the bones of extinct mammoths. No creature in the People's experience matched the size of those bones, so they surmised that the bones belonged to the Great Cannibal Owl, a malicious entity that carried off human children in the night. The Great Cannibal Owl was said to live in a cave in the Wichita Mountains, an alluring range of granite, laced with streams and abandoned gold mines, that rises as light as a cloud from the Oklahoma grasslands. The country around the Wichitas has a hallowed, ancestral feel to it, but when you drive through it with a Comanche, you cannot shake the feeling that it is, like the rest of Comancheria, a paradise lost.

"Our Comanche people don't like owls," Hammond Motah said as he drove around the base of the Wichitas, listening to the muffled bombardment from Fort Sill's vast gunnery range. "They're taboo. If my wife and I are at home at night and we hear a screech owl outside, we'll run out and chase it away."

Motah managed the print shop at the Comanche Tribal Complex and also served as the tribe's public information officer. He wore slacks and gray suspenders, and though he was fluent in PR jargon (he spoke frequently of the need to "develop a format" for my inquiries), the more time I spent with him the more I was convinced that his worldliness was only a veneer. In his late forties, Motah had the classic physiognomy of a Comanche: a stout body and a broad, powerful, contemplative face.

Motah studied elementary education at Arizona State, but he taught only briefly, working instead as a planner for other Plains tribes in the northern states. He came home to Oklahoma as something of an activist (he was one of the Comanches who took over the complex), and he had been deeply impressed by the cultural cohesion he had seen up north. It was a source of great sorrow to him that Comanche traditions seemed to be helplessly slipping away, replaced by a cultural crazy quilt stitched together with borrowings from other tribes. That is, arguably, the inevitable course of any society, but the Comanches were particularly vulnerable. As raiders and nomads they traveled light; they carried their culture in their heads. Their beliefs and manners were existential, rooted in action. Without the sustaining momentum of the open range, they began to collapse.

"We're really a vanishing race," Motah said. There was a tear forming in his eye. The Comanche language was dying out. People Motah's age could understand it but could not speak it fluently, and within another generation or so it would be a ceremonial relic like Latin. Young people beginning to dance in powwows were susceptible to fads and fashions, forsaking the old Comanche dances and taking up the single bustles of the northern tribes. Instead of sitting up all night cross-legged at a peyote meeting, singing the old songs and invoking the old spirits, kids tended to hang out in the parking lot after powwows, drinking and smoking dope. Soon, even the definition of a Comanche would have to be revised. Intermarriage among the tribes had been so common since the reservation days that 80 percent of the younger Comanches have no more than one fourth Comanche blood. If they marry someone with less than the minimum blood quantum—a likely occurrence— their children won't be Comanches. "This is the last generation," Kenneth Saupitty had told me, "that our constitution will allow."

Motah himself was married to a Kiowa, and though he and his in-laws got along fine, there were certain Kiowa taboos he had to watch out for. He could not speak directly to his mother-in-law, for example; if he did, his teeth would fall out.

"When it comes to the Kiowas," he told me, "I'm like a Man Called Horse."

Earlier that afternoon, Motah and I had visited the Comanche elder center in Lawton, where senior members of the tribe congregated every day for a free lunch. On the paneled walls were framed photographs of famous Comanches—Quanah with his implacable barbarian expression, Ten Bears in spectacles with a commemorative medallion around his neck. A few women in the front room were working at a quilting frame, but the rest of the elders were in the dining room, eating boiled hot dogs, sauerkraut, and canned beets. There were Halloween decorations on the tables. I sat down and talked for a while with an elder who reminisced about his childhood at the Fort Sill Indian School. He had arrived there terrified, not knowing a word of English. If you were caught speaking Comanche, he said, your mouth was washed out with soap.

Soon my attention was seized by a conversation at the far end of the table, where a woman was saying something about Adobe Walls.

"What'd you say?" an old man next to her asked. "Cement walls?"

"No, *Adobe*," she said and then turned to me. "You ever heard of Adobe Walls?"

"Yes, ma'am," I said. "In fact, I always wondered what happened to Ishatai. Do you know?"

"Who?"

"Ishatai."

"No, I don't know nothing about him."

After lunch we dropped in on a man named George "Woogee" Watchetaker, a former world champion pow-wow dancer ("I retired undefeated!"), artist, and rain-maker. Watchetaker was seventy-two. He had been born in a tent, back in the days when Comanches were still suspicious of houses and the bygone mores of the plains still had some sway. Back then, he remembered, Comanche men still plucked their eyebrows.

"My dad," he told us, "he made his own tweezers out of tin. He'd sharpen the tweezers with a file and pull his eyebrows out and his sideburns too."

Watchetaker himself had a trace of a moustache and a growth of stubble on his chin. He wore glasses with thick black frames and kept his hair in two long braids tied with rubber bands. He had few teeth. His living room was filled with souvenir-shop Indian art—plaster busts of braves and squaws, paintings of wide-eyed Indian children and mounted warriors praying to the Great Spirit.

"Here about 1969," he said, "I used to be a big drunkard. I used to smoke. The day before Christmas I got tired of it and wanted to quit. I went to bed and watched TV till midnight and then woke up at five-thirty, waiting for the TV to come on again. I was looking out that window when I saw something. It was a figure standing there. It looked like smoke. I wasn't scared or amazed at what I saw. Pretty soon it spoke to me— 'George, you know what you been doing is wrong. You got a short time to live. But if you change your way of life, you're gonna be well respected. You'll live a long time. Remember my words. Listen to me.'

"Then," Watchetaker said, making a snakelike motion with his hand, "he just slunk away. I didn't say anything to anybody about what I saw. That evening I played Santy Claus. My craving for drinking stopped just like that."

Not long after that incident, when West Texas was suffering under a drought, Watchetaker was asked to come to Wichita Falls and make rain. He had never professed to be a medicine man and was afraid to put himself on the line, but the spirit spoke to him again and told him to go ahead and try. He went to Wichita Falls, set a bowl of water down in the middle of a shopping-center parking lot, blessed it, smoked over it, and spit water in the four directions.

"And it hadn't been a minute before a bolt of lightning shot across the sky and it started raining. Next day they had big headlines: He done it.

"So I remember the words that that vision has told me," Watchetaker concluded. "I don't drink, I don't smoke, and my name has been everywhere."

That night there was a moon—a Comanche moon, bright enough to light the warpath—shining on the fields as we drove back to Lawton. Motah told me about the time, a few years back, when he had decided to go on a vision quest. In the bygone days a vision quest was the classic Comanche rite of manhood. A teenage boy would go out into the wilderness, deprive himself of food and water for four days and nights, and wait for his "visitor," usually an animal spirit who would issue instructions and leave the boy with a personal fund of mystical power—his medicine.

For his vision quest, Motah picked a site near a spring and made a circle of sage. He remembers being strong and confident the first day, but by the second day he was so thirsty he could not refrain from licking the dew off some nearby leaves. After a time his parents, both of whom had died years before, appeared to him pleading. "You don't have to do this," they said. "Come with us." But he stayed in the circle. He was taunted by a group of *nenuhpee*, sinister apparitions that take the form of tiny warriors and are also known to modern Comanches as leprechauns. "You're a fake," the *nenuhpee* jeered. "You don't belong here. You don't know anything about the old ways." Several more visitors appeared—some benign, some malevolent—but before the prescribed four nights had passed Motah was so hungry and sick and scared that he crawled out of the circle.

"I went home and slept for two days," he said. "I went to see a medicine man to tell him about my experience. He was extremely interested. He said he hadn't heard of a Comanche going on a vision quest for fifty years."

At the Comanche elder center I had been introduced to Thomas Wahnee, a seventy-seven-year-old retired roofer who was born, he told me, the year Quanah Parker died. Wahnee was a quiet, modest man who gave the impression of being subtly amused by everything he saw. He wore dark glasses and a hearing aid, and a single incisor dangled precariously from his upper jaw. Wahnee was a peyote man. Like many other elders, he had grown up in the Native American Church, attending meetings back in the days when participants still wore buckskin shirts and tied their braids with otter fur. Not all Comanches, of course, followed the peyote road. Most adhered to some variant of traditional Christian worship, while others found spiritual expression by participating in powwows. But the Comanches were the first Plains Indians to acquire the peyote religion, and they played a major role in its dissemination.

Wahnee invited me to attend a meeting of the church, and one cold winter evening I arrived at his house. A growly pit bull was chained up at the side of the house, and in the back yard a tepee stood next to a stock fence.

Ten people, mostly men in their sixties, had gathered for the meeting, and we sat around in Wahnee's house until late in the evening listening to tales of power and witchcraft and medicine. When the fire was built, Wahnee and the elder men led the way into the tepee, carrying their toolboxes (containing gourds and feather fans and other paraphernalia for the peyote rite) like men going off to work a late-night shift at a factory. We circled the outside of the tepee and then went inside and sat down on sofa cushions on a bed of sage.

Wahnee, as the leader, sat to the west of the earthen fire ring. The fire ring was in the shape of a crescent, the ends pointing east. In classic peyote symbology, the crescent represented the path of a man's life from birth to death, but over the years the religion had taken on an admixture of Christianity, and the shape of the fire ring now symbolized, as well, the hoofprint of the donkey that Jesus rode into Jerusalem.

When everyone was settled, Wahnee brought out the sacrament—Father Peyote—and placed it on the fire ring. It was a gray, wrinkly nubbin of cactus, ugly with knowledge and medicine. Wahnee then passed around corn shucks and a bag of Bull Durham tobacco, the makings of the ceremonial cigarettes that were to be smoked during the evening's first prayers. After the smoking and the praying Wahnee distributed a leather bag of peyote buttons and a vial of peyote powder. I ate one button and swallowed some of the powder, afterward rubbing my hands over my head and body as the ritual mandated. The bitter taste almost made me gag and the peyote sat uneasily in my stomach, but I began to gaze contentedly at the perfect glowing coals of the fire.

Then the singing began. Wahnee sang four songs, holding a staff and eagle feather in one hand and shaking a gourd with the other. He was accompanied by a drummer who pounded out a stern rhythm on a No. 6 cast-iron kettle that had been half filled with water and hot coals and then covered with a taut deer hide. Thus constructed, the drum was a little model of Mother Earth herself, a reverberant fusion of water and fire.

When Wahnee had finished with his songs he handed the staff and gourd and eagle feather to the man on his left. Each participant sang four songs, and when the circle was completed they began again and then again. It went on for five or six hours. I stared at the fire, trying to locate some sort of tonal entree into the music, but all the songs sounded indistinguishable to me. Nevertheless, I felt bound up in them somehow, and when each one ended I experienced a tiny wave of sadness along with the sensation that the temperature in the tepee had dropped a few degrees.

At two in the morning Wahnee sang the midnight song—about a band of Comanches long ago who had lost their horses and, while walking along a creek, killed a bear—and then he left the tepee to blow his cane whistle. He blew the whistle in each of the four directions, announcing to the world our prayerful presence there in the tepee. The notes he produced were so sharp and resonant it seemed that they were reaching us from the rim of the earth and that Wahnee himself had been transformed into some sort of magic bird.

When he came back he walked clockwise around the fire and took his seat again in front of Father Peyote. The singing and praying began again and went on for another three hours. At the next interval I asked Wahnee, according to protocol, for permission to leave the tepee for a moment. He nodded his head good-naturedly, and I stood up and made the circle to the east, taking care not to make the mistake of passing in front of anyone who was smoking and eating peyote. The fireman held the flap open for me as I walked out into the night, the songs commencing again behind me. The night was very cold and the sky was clear. There was dew on the grass and it glistened in the starlight. I was not supposed to go back into the tepee until there was a pause in the singing, so for a long time I just stood there and watched it. The tepee's canvas skin was transparent, and the fire pulsed inside it like a beating heart, in time to the drum and the voices.

I wondered for how much longer such vibrant remnants of the old Comanche life would endure. During the time I spent in Oklahoma I kept hearing about someone who, at least in theory, seemed perfectly poised between the Comanche past and the Comanche future. He was a great-grandson of Quanah Parker, and he had gone to Hollywood on a "sacred mission" to make a movie about his ancestor.

I met Vincent Parker for dinner at Chaya Brasserie near Beverly Hills. He would not tell me his age ("That's my secret," he said defiantly. "I have held on to that one little sense of mystery"), but he looked about thirty. He was wearing a Giorgio Armani suit with a matching tie and pocket square, and he carried a topcoat draped over his arm. His olive skin was smooth, and his hair was fashionably long and tousled.

Sipping a glass of red wine, he studied the menu. "I think I'll have the shrimp ravioli," he told the waiter. "The only problem is I hate to change wines."

Parker closed the menu and regarded me with an emphatic gaze, blinking incessantly, as if there was something wrong with his contacts. "I'm a living example of what Quanah Parker wanted," he said. "I am in some respects what he envisioned for his people. He wanted them not only to retain their identity but also to be at ease in this dominant society."

Vincent said he was the great-grandson of Quanah and Chony, the chief's first or second wife, depending on which scholar's opinion you accept. He had grown up in Lawton in a family with eleven brothers and sisters. His parents—who had the good fortune to strike oil on their allotted land—instilled in their children the Parker ambition to master the white man's world.

Vincent graduated from the University of Oklahoma, worked for a time as an aide to Oklahoma governor George Nye, and dabbled in tribal politics, running unsuccessfully for vice chairman after the 1980 takeover. He was keenly aware that his ancestor presided over all his endeavors.

"I told my father I felt different from any of my brothers and sisters. My father said, 'You *are* different. When I look at you, I see *him*.'"

That was powerful medicine. To a Parker, Quanah was hardly a typical mortal.

"He was a way-shower," Vincent said as the waiter brought his shrimp ravioli. "The Christians had their Jesus, the Indians had their Gandhi, and the Comanches had their Quanah Parker."

Vincent had the feeling that he was meant to be a way-shower, but wasn't sure how he was to accomplish it. He spent a lot of time in the Star House, Quanah's famous residence, sitting in his great-grandfather's chair and praying for guidance. One night his mission came to him: He would write and produce a play about Quanah. He secluded himself in the Star House to write the script, and when it was finished he blessed it by fanning cedar smoke over it with an eagle feather. Nine months later, the play premiered as an outdoor pageant in Quanah, Texas, with members of the Parker family making up the cast. The pageant ran for five years, and then Vincent moved to Los Angeles to pursue the goal of commemorating Quanah in a feature film. Bankrolled by his family, he traveled west with a sense of sacred purpose and a wish list. ("Before I left Oklahoma," he said, "I wrote in my journal that I wanted a Gucci watch. I love black and gold. The first day in L.A., I went to Gucci and bought it.")

During his time in L.A. Vincent has worked in various postproduction positions for Walt Disney Studios, learning the industry to prepare himself for his task. With his remarkable tenacity and focus, he has already begun to beat the odds. A documentary on Quanah that he produced has just been completed, and he has come close to putting together the funding for a feature. In his spare time he has dabbled in modeling and has been hired to appear in a commercial for Jeep Comanche, in which he will face the camera and say, "Comanches. My forefathers led them. Now I drive them."

"Sometimes it's hard," he said. "I'll call my father and tell him I have no energy. I get tired of playing the social circuit, putting up with the Hollywood bullshit. At any given moment I question it. I can understand how Jesus wept and questioned his own mission."

On the other hand, it's not so terrible. "Going to dinner at Spago, Le Dome, and Nicky Blair's. That's my world. I love the wonderful cultural activities that are afforded to me here. People laugh at me because I spend so much time at Tiffany's, but there are so many wonderful things there! I give no apologies for being driven in a chauffeured limousine. Quanah himself had a surrey with silver trim. If he were here today he'd be with me in the limo. What made him effective is the spiritual influence he brought about. If anything, that's what I'm trying to hold on to."

After dinner we walked down the street, toward the Beverly Center, talking about the Adobe Walls song that Quanah had written after the battle and that was one of the few surviving Comanche songs from pre-reservation days. It was a song of mourning, a song of loss.

"I do intend to protect the integrity of this project at all costs," Vincent said, returning to the movie. "I tell producers, 'You're going to continue your careers in L.A.

I'm not. I'm going back to these people in Oklahoma, and no amount of money could compensate me for the damage I could do. I cannot sell out!'"

I stared frankly at this improbable person. He may have been just another Hollywood hustler with a messiah complex, but I didn't think so. Beneath his fashion plate exterior, there was something steely about him, and it was not hard to imagine him in another time as an arrogant and fearless warrior, a lord of the plains.

"I'm not playing around out here," he said with sudden passion, as the Beverly Hills traffic surged by us. "I'm on the warpath."

The Temple of Destiny

In 1519—almost half a millennium ago—two men stood at the top of a temple pyramid in the Valley of Mexico, looking out over the Aztec city of Tenochtitlán. Both men were in the grip of a dream. Hernán Cortés was thirty-four years old, a tall, lithe gentleman-adventurer from the Spanish province of Extremadura. His hair was thin and his beard too sparse to completely conceal a knife scar near his upper lip. Though his physical and mental energies were boundless, he had the complexion of a scribe. ("Their bodies were as white as the new buds of the cane stalk," the Aztecs marveled of the Spaniards, "as white as the buds of the maguey.") Ever since Cortés and his five hundred followers had sailed from Cuba for the unknown shores of Mexico, they had been riding a tide of fabulous luck, and now the tide had delivered them to the dreamscape of Tenochtitlán, to this beautiful and gruesome city floating like a water hyacinth in the middle of a lake.

Montezuma II, the ruler of the Aztecs, was fifty-two. In his youth he had been an honored warrior, but as emperor he was a rarefied being, a pitiless aesthete who dined on young children and fretted over every uncertain portent. For a long time there had been plenty of worrisome signs: a comet, "like a flaming ear of corn"; a strange storm in the lake; a captured bird with a mirror in the center of its head. All of this had helped to convince

Montezuma that Cortés was the incarnation of Quetzalcóatl, the banished god whose vengeful return had long been prophesied. Montezuma was terrified of Quetzalcóatl, who promised to depose Huitzilopochtli, the Hummingbird on the Left, the god of war and human sacrifice from whom the emperor derived his power. But Montezuma could not fight a god, and so his only choice was to welcome the intruder with wary courtesy. "No, it is not a dream," he told Cortés at their first meeting. "I am not walking in my sleep. . . . I have seen you at last! I have met you face to face!"

Montezuma was not asleep, but even at this distance the conquest of Mexico seems more dream than history, some abiding pageant of the unconscious mind. Ever since I first read, over ten years ago, that Mexico City utility workers had discovered the remains of the Great Temple, I had been mad to go there, to see with my own eyes the evidence that this amazing story had really taken place. Could there be a more resonant tourist attraction anywhere in the New World? Here, at the summit of this pyramid, Cortés and Montezuma had stood for a moment hand in hand, and then a few months later the uneasy stasis was broken forever and the idol of Huitzilopochtli was carried down the steep steps, its place in the temple reclaimed by a statue of the Virgin.

Within a matter of months Montezuma was dead, and though Cortés and his followers were forced to flee the city in mortal chaos, they came back a year later to erase it from the earth. They pulled down the pyramid along with the seventy-odd other buildings that had once formed the main ceremonial complex of the Aztecs. The ruins and foundations of those buildings—palaces and temples, monasteries, idol houses where sacrificial victims were dismembered and stewed, a royal zoo and aviary that employed three hundred keepers—were buried beneath the Christian streets. Mexico City's main plaza was superimposed squarely upon the site of Aztec religious and civic life. The city of Tenochtitlán had not entirely vanished, but its shattered remains lay secreted away.

Today the ruins of the pyramid are exposed, and a splendid new museum that interprets the history of the Great Temple rises discreetly behind them. At first glance, visitors might easily mistake the site for an unfinished public works project. The greater part of the pyramid was destroyed, and its base, like so many other buildings in Mexico City—like the immense listing cathedral fifty yards away—has subsided into the soft ground reclaimed over the centuries from Lake Texcoco. Where once the pyramid was a towering monument, it is now a depression in the earth, an expanse of truncated walls and corridors made of volcanic stones, its decorative stucco facade long since eroded away. Visitors' catwalks lead down from the street and over the unpolished marble floors of ancient plazas and temples and ceremonial quarters. Pieces of massive sculpture are still visible: boxy, snub-nosed serpents' heads, so stylized they look mechanical; grim-faced frogs crouched like sentinels; a wall carving of human skulls.

The ruins represent a complicated process of building and renovation. During the two hundred years of Aztec residence in Tenochtitlán the pyramid was periodically enlarged, and each new phase was built on top of the one preceding it. Much of what is exposed today would have been hidden in Cortés' time; he would have seen only the final phase, the tallest and grandest pyramid the Aztecs ever built, crowned at its summit by massive temples to Huitzilopochtli and Tlaloc, the god of rain.

Bernal Diaz, who was with Cortés and whose chronicles of his adventures are precise and vivid, recalled that the Spaniards climbed 114 steps to reach the top of the pyramid. Once there, Montezuma turned to Cortés and expressed concern that his visitors must be exhausted from the ascent. Cortés replied that he and his men were never tired.

From the temple platform Montezuma showed the Spaniards the view. Tenochtitlán was built on an island in the middle of Lake Texcoco, creating an ingenious imperial fortress connected to the mainland by three causeways whose access was controlled with removable bridges. There were other cities along the mainland shore, and Diaz could see their temples in the distance "like gleaming white towers and castles: a marvelous sight." Montezuma pointed out the aqueduct, which brought fresh water from the springs at Chapultépec, and the canoe traffic flowing along the surface of the lake and through the extensive network of inner-city canals. The Spaniards could hear, from miles away, the murmur of commerce in the central market whose size and splendor eclipsed any they had seen in Europe.

And yet in the eyes of Cortés and his men it was all built upon an abomination. Though they themselves had slaughtered thousands of innocents on their march through Mexico, they could neither comprehend nor tolerate the idea of ritualized human sacrifice. To the Aztecs and the other nations of Mexico, however, sacrifice was a binding tenet of existence. The gods constantly required the nourishment of "precious eagle-cactus fruit"—the pumping human hearts ripped from the bodies of living victims. When the Great Temple was consecrated in 1487, tens of thousands of people—taken by the Aztecs in war or as tribute—were sacrificed. For four days the procession of victims made its way up the steps, as visiting dignitaries watched from galleries that were garlanded with flowers and sedge to protect against the reek of gore. In front of the Hummingbird's temple the priests would seize each victim and bend him backward until his body was as taut as a bow, then the executioner would slice beneath the ribs with a ceremonial knife and in the next motion reach in and tear out the wildly beating heart. The body was then rolled down the stairs, along a stream of blood that made its way down the pyramid in a slow cataract. At the bottom, the limbs were cut off to be cooked with squash for a ritual human feast, and the torsos were tossed to the animals in the zoo.

On their journey to Tenochtitlán the Spaniards had already seen their share of human sacrifice; along the way they had been toppling idols and converting the native priests into acolytes after washing the matted blood out of their hair. Cortés and his men were cruel and hardened adventurers, but they seem to have been genuinely unnerved by the idolatrous bloodlust they saw all around them. Their mission of conquest and greed steadily deepened into a religious crusade. Isolated in a world as unbelievable as a distant planet, they clung desperately to their idols, no doubt realizing that in this dangerous city the subtlest turn of events could place the invaders themselves on the sacrificial slabs.

On the pyramid that day Cortés asked to be allowed inside the temple, and after some thought and consultation the emperor led the Spaniards into the sanctum of Huitzilopochtli. His guests were horrified. The idol of the Hummingbird, Diaz reported, had "huge terrible eyes." Three human hearts were burning in a brazier, and "the walls of that shrine were so splashed and caked with blood that they and the floor too were black. Indeed, the whole place stank abominably. . . . The stench was worse than any slaughterhouse in Spain."

Cortés asked Montezuma for permission to erect a cross on the top of the pyramid, so that the lord of the Aztecs could see how his false idols would tremble in the presence of the true God. Montezuma replied, "in some temper," that if he had known Cortés was going to offer such insults he would never have allowed him into the temple.

Cortés tactfully dropped the subject. Montezuma's hospitality was icy, but it was all that was keeping Cortés and his men alive. Over the next week or so it became clear to the Spaniards just how precarious their situation was. Montezuma protected them only because he thought Cortés was Quetzalcóatl, and he dared not challenge a god. But Montezuma's control over the situation was shaky. There were thousands of Aztec warriors—Jaguar and Eagle knights armed with wooden broadswords faced with cutting edges of obsidian—who had very little tolerance for their uninvited guests. Cortés' predicament was delicate, but his response was astonishingly blunt: He arrested Montezuma in the heart of his own capital.

This outrageous strategy worked for a time. Montezuma was dumbfounded and ashamed, but compliant with the will of Quetzalcóatl. Diaz tells us that the Spaniards treated him with great deference, that during the long, idle hours of his house arrest the emperor argued religion with Cortés and gambled good-naturedly at a game played with smooth gold pellets. "It was not necessary to instruct most of us," Diaz writes, "about the civility that was due to this great chief."

Cortés was now the dictator of a restive Tenochtitlán, and with typical bravado he marched to the top of the pyramid—to the temple of Huitzilopochtli—with an iron bar in his hand. "Upon my word as a gentleman," wrote one of Cortés' soldiers many years later, "I can still see him as he leaped high in the air, hovering over us almost supernaturally as he smashed the iron bar down on the idol's head."

"Who would conquer Tenochtitlán?" reads a fragment of Aztec poetry engraved on a wall of the new Museum of the Great Temple. "Who could shake the foundation of heaven?" The museum itself is filled with artifacts found at the site. The most arresting is a nine-ton monolithic oval disk, bearing in low relief the image of Coyolxauhqui, the treacherous goddess who was killed by her brother Huitzilopochtli when he was born, fully armed, from beneath the writhing serpent skirts of his mother. The dismembered goddess is depicted on the stone as a jumble of body parts, the head angled away from the torso, the limbs sheathed in armor studded with the likenesses of rattlesnakes. Not far from this violent and chaotic sculpture I came upon a seashell carved from a boulder, a work of such finesse and serenity that it instantly shattered my old storybook notions about the ferocious gloom of Aztec thought. The shell's beauty was troublesome, and challenging. Who were they, after all, these people who chose the harmless, radiant humming-bird as the manifestation of the deadliest god humankind has ever worshipped?

After an hour or two of wandering through the museum—among the life-size terra-cotta statues of Eagle Knights, the displays of sacrificial knives, the human skulls with leering stone eyes set into the sockets—I was

no closer to an answer than when I came in, and the story of the Aztecs and their conquest by Cortés still seemed like a supernatural event. It was hard to view the story through the eyes of a historian, as a military campaign beset by the usual run of confusion, intrigue, and complicated alliances. On some level Montezuma's perception made more sense: the conquest of Mexico was a clash of gods whose fatal outcome had long since been preordained.

On the first floor of the museum I stopped in front of a model of the Great Temple. The pyramid was depicted along with the scores of other buildings that made up the center of Tenochtitlán. The complex was surrounded by a high wall known as Coatepantli, the Serpent Wall, and the buildings within the enclosure looked sterile and polished. Little human figures had been positioned around the grounds, and when I looked closely I could see lords in their feathered headdresses, armed knights in the guise of their animal totems. The pyramid dominated everything, towering and steep, its walls studded with the stone heads of serpents. The exhibit had the placid unreality of a model railroad layout, but it was still startling to realize that a city like this had once existed.

That city was gone, of course, cursed and obliterated by the conquering Spaniards. That Cortés and his men survived to wreak such vengeance is one of history's miracles. The arrest of Montezuma had only forestalled the crisis that was building in the city. Cortés was weakening, and he was surrounded by a hostile population that had lost faith in the credibility of the emperor. Finally, when it seemed an attack by the inhabitants was imminent, Cortés persuaded Montezuma to climb onto the palace roof and tell his people to let the Spaniards leave the city in peace. As the lord of the Aztecs stood there in his embroidered mantle and turquoise earplugs, his bottom lip pierced with a crystal tube containing the feather of a kingfisher, he was met with a hail of stones. One of the stones hit him in the head, and when he was brought back to his apartments, he refused all ministrations and languished, as Diaz tells it, until he died.

"Cortés and all of us captains and soldiers wept for him," Diaz says, though some historians believe that the Spaniards, angered by how useless the emperor had become to them, stabbed him to death on their way out of the city.

The Spanish memorialized their retreat from Tenochtitlán as La Noche Triste, the Night of Sorrow. More than half of Cortés' men perished in this nightmarish battle, and none escaped unwounded. Hacking their way along a causeway, the Spanish were pressed on all sides by thousands of warriors in canoes. The Aztecs removed the bridges in the causeway; Cortés' men fell into the gaps and drowned from the weight of the gold they were carrying, forming new bridges of dead men and horses across which other soldiers made their way to the mainland.

The Aztecs thought they had driven the Spaniards out forever, but the prophecy was still unfulfilled. Cortés managed to rally his men, enlist the aid of Tenochtitlán's enemies, and besiege the city a year later. He built ships and launched a navy on the lake, blockading the Aztec capital and subduing one by one the cities on the mainland that provided it support. Finally he assaulted Tenochtitlán itself. "Such was the slaughter done on water and on land," Cortés wrote to Charles V, "that with prisoners taken the enemy's casualties numbered in all more than 40,000 men. The shrieks and weeping of the women and children were so terrible that we felt our hearts breaking." When Cuauhtémoc, Montezuma's successor, was captured and brought before Cortés, he tearfully begged to be stabbed. Cortés refused, and patted him on the head.

Late one afternoon I took a walk from my hotel to the pyramid. I was staying at the Hotel de Cortés, a cool stone bulwark built in the eighteenth century as a home for Franciscan monks who had come to end their days in New Spain after a lifetime of missionary work in the Philippines. In front of the hotel ran Avenida Hidalgo, the street built along the route of the old Tacuba causeway, along which Cortés had fought his way out of the city on La Noche Triste.

I crossed the street and made my way through the alameda, the plaza where, after the conquest, the Spanish had burned infidels. Now it was a public park draped with willows and bordered by street vendors.

My way took me past the Palacio de Bellas Artes, the national concert hall, which was built in the 1930's and which has already sunk twelve feet into the substrate; through the colonial heart of the City of Mexico, with its sixteenth-century buildings housing banks and *pastelerias* and religious-supply shops where one could buy a statue of a bloodied Christ lying in a transparent casket like Sleeping Beauty; onto the zocalo, the main plaza, where a crowd of striking schoolteachers had assembled to listen to speeches and chant their demands.

It was a clear day for Mexico City, but I could taste the particulate in the air, and the demonstration reminded me of the city's desperate, sprawling essence: the 18 million souls who lived on the surface of the vanished lake, in the despoiled metropolis that spread over the once magical Valley of Mexico.

I walked into the Metropolitan Cathedral, which the Spanish began building in 1573 as a monument to the bloody exorcism that Cortés had conducted in Tenochtitlán. The cathedral was vast and heavy; I could sense its weight. It was not vaulting toward heaven but pressing down upon the earth. The floor was uneven, moving upward toward the nave like a ramp. Everywhere there were altars and chapels, lofts and pulpits, golden encrustations. It was a gloomy place that spoke of the vengeance of the Lord, the heartless triumph of Quetzalcóatl. Here, where the cathedral was erected, where images of tortured saints now resided, had stood the great cranial racks of the Aztecs, the skulls of sacrificial victims strung like beads on an abacus—so many skulls, says Diaz, that it was impossible to count.

When I came out of the cathedral, the teachers had begun to disperse. Vendors were selling comic books and mangoes on sticks, the flesh carved like rose petals. Over by the Great Temple a line of salesmen had set out blankets for displaying their wares. One man had an ancient set of bathroom scales on which a customer could weigh himself for a few pesos. Another demonstrated wind-up plastic scorpions. A boy stood trying to interest passersby in two baby squirrels that skittered along on the pavement, their necks secured by leashes made of string.

The squirrels were so small and so out of place that for a moment they startled me, as if they were some new kind of creature. But they were just one more lingering, exotic element, part of the strangeness that Cortés had finally been unable to quell. Mexico City itself seemed that way, exotic and forlorn. "My heart burns and suffers," Montezuma had said, "as if it were drowned in spices . . ."

I stood at the railing of the excavation and looked down upon the volcanic building blocks and the weathered serpents' heads with their thick ribbons of flicking tongues. I could see braziers and four-petaled flowers carved into the stone, and the remains of the apartments where the Eagle Knights had once gathered to put on their feathered ceremonial dress. They had stood here; it had all happened. Cortés destroyed the pyramid, but he could not eradicate its foundations. And it was fitting, I thought, that the city of Tenochtitlán was now underground, half-glimpsed but silently persisting, like some dark but enticing thought that cannot be banished from the mind.

The Soul of Treaty Oak

According to Stephen Redding, a mystical arborist who lived on a farm in Pennsylvania called Happy Tree, the Treaty Oak expired at 5:30 in the afternoon on Tuesday, July 25, 1989. Redding felt the tree's soul leave its body. He heard its last words—"Where are my beloved children?"

Redding had read about the bizarre plight of the Treaty Oak in the *Philadelphia Inquirer*, and he had come to Austin to help ease the tree's suffering, to be with it in its terrible hour. The Treaty Oak by that time was an international celebrity. People in London, Tokyo, and Sydney had heard the story of how Austin's massive, centuries-old live oak—once showcased in the American

Forestry Association's Tree Hall of Fame—had been *poisoned*; how a feed-store employee named Paul Cullen allegedly had poured a deadly herbicide called Velpar around the base of the tree in patterns that suggested some sort of occult mischief. It was an act of vandalism that the world immediately perceived as a sinister and profound crime. As the Treaty Oak stood there, helplessly drawing Velpar through its trunk and limbs, it became an unforgettable emblem of our ruined and innocent earth.

Stephen Redding—a big man with dark swept-back hair and a fleshy, solemn face—was only one of many people who felt the tree calling out to them in anguish. Over the years Redding had been in and out of jail for various acts of civil disobedience on behalf of threatened trees, and he hinted darkly that the car wreck that had left him dependent on a walker may not have been an accident ("It was very mysterious—a dark night, a lonely intersection"). In preparation for his visit to the Treaty Oak, Redding fasted for six days, allowing himself only a teaspoon of maple syrup a day ("My means of partaking a little bit of the lifeblood of the tree kingdom"). On his second night in Austin, he put his hand on the tree's root flare and felt its slow pulse. He tied a yellow ribbon around its trunk and planted impatiens at its base. For almost a week he camped out under the tree, criticizing the rescue procedures that had been prescribed by a task force of foresters, plant pathologists, chemists, and arborists from all over the country. Finally Redding grew so pesty that the city decided to escort him away from the tree. That was when he felt it die.

"It was so intense," he told me in his hotel room a few days later. "I just kind of fell back on my cot without the energy even to sit. I felt like someone had dropped a sledge on my chest."

"I heard that you saw a blue flickering flame leave the tree," I said.

"I'd prefer not to speak about that. If you want to enter the rumor, that's okay. I don't want to confirm it. You could suggest that rumor has it that it looked like a coffee cup steaming. And if the rumor also said there was a hand on the loop of the coffee cup you could say that too."

I was surprised to realize, after an hour or so of hearing Redding expound upon the feelings of trees and the secret harmony of all living things, that I was listening not just with my usual journalist's detachment but with a kind of hunger. Anyone who went by to pay respects to the Treaty Oak in the last few months would recognize that hunger: a need to understand how the fate of this stricken tree could move and outrage us so deeply, how it could seem to call to each of us so personally.

When I read about the poisoning, I took my children by to see Treaty Oak, something I had never thought to do when it was in good health. The tree stands in its own little park just west of downtown Austin. Although in its present condition it is droopy and anemic, with its once-full leaf canopy now pale and sparse, it is still immense. It has the classic haunted shape of a live oak—the contorted trunk, the heavy limbs bending balefully down to the earth, the spreading crown overhead projecting a pointillistic design of light and leaf shadow.

The historical marker in front of the tree perpetuates the myth that Stephen F. Austin signed a treaty with a tribe of Indians—Tonkawas or Comanches—beneath its branches. The marker also states that the tree is six hundred years old, an educated guess that may exaggerate the truth by two hundred years or so. But the tree is certainly older than almost any other living thing in Texas, and far older than the idea of Texas itself. Stephen F. Austin may not have signed his treaty beneath the Treaty Oak, but even in his time it was already a commanding landmark. According to another legend, the tree served as a border marking the edge of early Austin. Children were told by their mothers they could wander only as far as Treaty Oak. Beyond the tree was Indian country.

It was a cool evening in early June when we went by Treaty Oak that first time. I looked down at the kids as they looked up at the tree and thought that this moment had the potential to become for them one of those childhood epiphanies that leave behind, in place of hard memory, a mood or a shadowy image that would pester them all their lives. The several dozen people who had gathered around the tree that evening were subdued, if not downright heartsick. This thing had hit Austin hard. In its soul Austin is a druid capital, a city filled with sacred trees and pools and stones, all of them crying out for protection. When my neighborhood supermarket was built, for instance, it had to be redesigned to accommodate a venerable old pecan tree, which now resides next to the cereal section in a foggy glass box. Never mind that Austin had been rapaciously destroying its environment for years. The *idea* of trees was still enshrined in the civic bosom. In Austin an assault on a tree was not just a peculiar crime; it was an unspeakable crime, a blasphemy.

"Oh, poor thing," a woman said as she stood in front of the ailing oak. Like everyone else there, she seemed to regard the tree as if it were a sick puppy rather than an implacable monument of nature. But you could not help personifying it that way. The tree's inanimate being—its very *lack* of feeling—only made it seem more helpless. Someone had left flowers at its base, and there were a few cards and brave efforts at poems lying about, but there was nowhere near the volume of weird get-well tokens that would come later. On the message board that had been set up, my children added their sentiments. "Get well Treaty Oak," my seven-year-old daughter wrote. "From a big fan of you."

Would it live? The answer depended on the experts you asked, and on their mood at the time. "The Treaty Oak was an old tree before this happened," John Giedraitis, Austin's urban forester, told me as we stood at the base of the tree a few days after Stephen Redding had declared it dead. "It's like an old lady in a nursing home who falls down and breaks her hip. She may survive, but she'll never be the same afterward."

Giedraitis was sipping from a Styrofoam cup half filled with coffee. "If this were a cup of Velpar," he said, holding it up, "about half of the liquid that's in here would have been enough to kill the tree. We think this guy used a whole gallon."

The Treaty Oak poisoning had thrust Giedraitis from his workaday position in an unsung city bureaucracy into a circus of crisis management. His passionate way of speaking had served him well in countless television interviews, and now when he walked down the street in Austin, people turned to him familiarly to inquire about the welfare of the tree. He replied usually in guarded language, in a tone of voice that betrayed his own emotional attachment to the patient. Two years earlier,

Giedraitis had proposed to his wife beneath Treaty Oak's branches.

"There was never any question in my mind that Treaty Oak was where I would propose," he said. "That's the power spot. That's the peace spot."

"This is a magnificent creature," he said, standing back to survey the ravaged tree with its startling network of life-support equipment. A series of screens fifty-five feet high guarded the tree from the sun and made the site look from a distance like a baseball stadium. A system of plastic pipe, carrying Utopia Spring Water donated by the company, snaked up its trunk, and every half hour the spring water would rain down upon the leaves.

"You know," Giedraitis went on, "it's hard to sit here over the last six weeks like I have and think it doesn't have some sort of spirit. You saw those roots. This thing is pressed to the earth. This thing is *alive*!"

Giedraitis said he thought the tree might have been poisoned as long as five months before the crime was discovered. He first noticed something wrong on March 2, when he took a group of visiting urban foresters to see Treaty Oak and happened to spot a few strips of dead grass near the tree. The dead grass was surprising but not particularly alarming—it was probably the result of a city employee's careless spraying of a relatively mild chemical edger at the base of the tree.

Treaty Oak seemed fine until the end of May, when a period of heavy rains caused the water-activated Velpar that was already soaking the roots of the tree to rise from its chemical slumber. On the Friday before Memorial Day weekend, Connie Todd, who worked across the street from the tree, noted with concern that its leaves were turning brown. She thought at first it must be oak wilt, which had been decimating the trees in her South Austin neighborhood. But when she looked closer at the leaves, she saw they were dying not from the vein out—the classic symptom of oak wilt—but from the edge inward. Todd called Giedraitis, who looked at the leaves and knew that the tree had been poisoned.

But by what, and by whom, and why? Whoever had applied the poison had poured it not only around the base of the tree but also in a peculiar half-moon pattern to the east. Giedraitis called in tree experts from Texas A&M University and the Texas Forest Service. Samples were taken from the soil to see what kind of poison had been used. Eight inches of topsoil were removed. Amazonian microbes and activated charcoal were injected into the ground.

When the lab reports came back on the poison, Giedraitis was stunned. Velpar! Velpar is the sort of scorched-earth herbicide that is used to eliminate plants and competing trees from pine plantations and Christmas-tree farms. Velpar does not harm most conifers, but it kills just about everything else. The chemical is taken up into a tree by its roots and travels eventually to the leaves, where it enters the chloroplasts and short-circuits the chemical processes by which photosynthesis is conducted. The tree's reaction to these nonfunctioning leaves is to cast them off and bring on a new set. But in a Velpar-infested tree, the new leaves will be poisoned too. The tree dies by starvation. It uses its precious reserves of energy to keep producing new leaves that are unable to fulfill their function of turning sunlight into food.

When Giedraitis and his colleagues discovered that Velpar was the poison, they immediately realized that Treaty Oak was in a desperate condition. As its tainted leaves fell to the ground and a deadly new crop emerged to replace them, outraged citizens called for the lynching of the unknown perpetrator from the very branches of the tree. They suggested that he be forced to drink Velpar. Du Pont, the maker of Velpar, offered a $10,000 reward for information leading to the conviction of the person who had so callously misused its product. The Texas Forestry Association chipped in another $1,000. Meanwhile a twenty-six-person task force bankrolled by H. Ross Perot convened in Austin and considered courses of treatment. The sun screens were erected, and the tree's upper branches were wrapped in burlap to prevent them from becoming overheated because of the loss of the leaf canopy overhead. Samples showed that the soil was contaminated to a depth of at least thirty-four inches, and so the dirt around the base of the tree was dug out, exposing the ancient roots that had bound the earth beneath the oak for hundreds of years. When the root system became too dense to dig through, the poisoned soil was broken with high-pressure hoses and sluiced away.

A Dallas psychic named Sharon Capehart, in Austin at the invitation of a local radio station, told Giedraitis that the workers had not dug far enough. The tree had spoken to her and told her what their samples confirmed—that there were still six inches of poisoned soil.

Capehart took off her shoes and crawled down into the hole and did a transfer of energy to the tree.

"It was a tremendous transfer," she told me. "But she needed it so much. It was like she was drawing it out of me."

Capehart had determined that Treaty Oak was a female. In another lifetime—when the tree was in human form—it had been Capehart's mother in ancient Egypt. The tree had a name, which it passed on to Capehart, stipulating that she could release it only to the person her spirit guides had revealed to her.

Meanwhile the vigil in front of the Treaty Oak continued. Sharon Capehart wasn't the only one beaming positive energy to the tree. To the protective chain that now cordoned off the Treaty Oak, visitors attached all sorts of get-well exotica: holy cards, photographs, feathers, poems ("Hundreds of you / Fall everyday / The lungs of the World, / by our hands taken down. / Forgive us ancient one"), even a movie pass to the Varsity Theatre, made out in the name of Treaty Oak. People had set coins into the brass letters of the historical marker, and on the ground before it were flowers, cans of chicken soup, crystals, keys, toys, crosses, everything from a plastic unicorn to a bottle of diarrhea medicine.

All of this was so typical of Austin. Looking at this array of talismans, I was convinced anew that Austin would always be the never-never land of Texas. What other city would take the plight of an assaulted tree so grievously to heart or come to its rescue with such whimsical resolve?

There was a suspect. Sharon Capehart had an intimation of a "sandy-haired gentleman with glasses, around the age of thirty-eight," and that was about what the police turned up, though the man was forty-five. His name, Paul Stedman Cullen, had been put forward to the police by several different informants. Paul Cullen worked in a feed store in the nearby suburb of Elroy and lived alone in a truck trailer, where he read science fiction and books on occult magic with solitary fervor. According to the police, his arrest record—for drunken driving, for drug possession, for burglary—dated back more than twenty years. He had lived in California in the sixties, during the salad days of the drug culture, and now he drove a truck with a sign in the rear window that read "Apollyon at the Wheel" and was a self-confessed member of the Aryan Brotherhood.

Paul Cullen had poisoned the tree, the informants told the police, because he wanted to entrap its spiritual energy to win the love of a woman or to ward off a rival. They described the poisonous circle he had drawn at the base of Treaty Oak and mentioned the books—including one called *The Black Arts*—that he might have used as ritualistic manuals.

"Any pagan knows better than to kill a tree," an outraged Austin pagan known as Bel told me. "And *The Black Arts* is nothing but metaphysical masturbation. The reaction of the pagan community to this act is one of disgust."

Before Cullen could be charged with a crime, the tree had to be coolly appraised, using a complicated formula devised by the Council of Tree and Landscape Appraisers. The formula takes into account a tree's species, location, condition, historical value, and trunk size. (According to the guidelines, the current value of a "perfect specimen shade tree" is $27 per square inch of trunk cross section: "The cross section area is determined by the formula $0.7854D$, where D equals the diameter measured.") When all the figures were applied, the mighty entity of Treaty Oak was judged to be worth $29,392.69. Because the tree's value was more than $20,000, Cullen was charged with second-degree felony mischief.

"It's tree worship!" Cullen's attorney, Richard C.

Jenkins, shouted at me over the phone as he proclaimed his client's innocence. "In my opinion, Paul is a political prisoner. He's being sacrificed in a new kind of witch-craft rite. He could go to jail for *life*! People have really jumped off the deep end on this one. Usually this kind of treatment is reserved for murder victims. Rape victims! Child-molestation victims! But a tree? Come on! I mean, it's a *tree*!"

Though the poisoned soil had been removed from the base of Treaty Oak, the tree was still full of Velpar, and the chemical crept slowly up its trunk and branches, killing off the leaves flush by flush. As a last desperate measure, the tree scientists drilled holes in the trunk of the tree and injected thirty-five gallons of a weak potas-sium-chloride solution, hoping that this salty flood would help the tree purge itself of the poison.

Sharon Capehart, in Abilene for a radio talk show, felt the tree weeping and calling out to her for another energy transfer. As soon as she was able, she got in her car and headed toward Austin. "Around Georgetown I could really feel her weeping and wanting me to hurry hurry. I told her, 'Just wait. I'm putting the pedal to the metal. I'm getting there.'"

Capehart arrived at Treaty Oak wearing high heels, a tight black skirt, and a red jacket. Her blond hair was teased in a manner that made it look as if it were flaring in the wind. There were four or five other women with her, students and assistants, and they made a circle around the tree, holding out their hands and drawing the negative energy—the Velpar itself—into their bodies and then releasing it into the atmosphere. I was told I would be able to smell the poison leaving the tree, and I did detect an ugly gassy smell that may have been Velpar or may have been fumes from the Chevrolet body shop next door.

Capehart and her team did one transfer and then took a break, smoking cigarettes and waiting for their bodies to recharge their stores of positive energy.

During the second transfer the women each held a limb of the tree, and then they all converged on the trunk, laying their hands flat against the bark. Capehart's head jerked back and forth, and she swayed woozily as a couple of squirrels skittered around the trunk of the tree just above her head.

"Are we doing it, or what?" she called from the tree in triumph. "Two squirrels!"

Capehart's spirit guides had told her that I was the person to whom she should reveal the name of the tree. "Your name was given to me before you ever called," she told me in her hotel room after the transfer. "They let me know you'd try to understand."

She dabbed at her lipstick with a paper napkin and tapped the ash off her cigarette.

"Her name is Alexandria," she said. "Apparently Alexander the Great had started the city of Alexandria in the Egyptian days, and she was named after that. She was of royalty. She had jet-black hair, coal-black, very shiny. She was feminine but powerful. She had slate-blue eyes and a complexion like ivory."

Alexandria had been through many lifetimes, Capehart said, and had ended up as a tree, an unusual development.

"None of the guides or spirits I've communicated with have ever come up in a plant form before," Capehart said. "This is my first as far as plant life goes."

The energy transfer, she said, had gone well. Alexandria had told Capehart that when she began to feel better, she would drop her leaves upon the psychic's crown chakra. Sure enough, as Capehart stood at the base of the tree, she felt two leaves fall onto her head.

"There ain't no way that tree is dead. That spirit has not left that tree. She is a high-level being. They never leave without letting everybody notice."

Entrusted with the name of the tree, I felt compelled to visit it once again. She—I could not help but think of it as a female now—did not look to me as if she could ever recover. There was a fifth flush of poisoned leaves now, and the tree's branches seemed saggy and desiccated. There was not much cause for optimism. At the very best, if Treaty Oak survived, it would not be nearly the tree it had once been.

But even in its ravaged state it remained a forceful presence, a hurt and beckoning thing that left its visitors mute with reverence. And the visitors still came, leaving cards and crystals and messages. All of the attention paid to the tree had created, here and there, a discordant backlash. An anti-abortion crusader had left a prophecy, saying that, because of all the babies "slaughtered without mercy" by the city of Austin, "the tree that she loved will wither and die. Tho' she care for it night and day forever, that tree will not survive." Others complained, in letters to the editor, in press conferences, in editorials, that the money and resources that had been bestowed on the tree should have been used for the poor, the mentally ill, the Indians. They saw the circus surrounding the tree as a sign of cruel indifference, as if this spontaneous display of concern subtracted from, rather than added to, the world's store of human sympathy.

I talked for a while to a man named Ed Bustin, who

had lived across the street from Treaty Oak for years and who used to climb it as a boy, working his way up its steady branches to its spreading summit. Another neighbor, Gordon Israel, had gathered up some of Treaty Oak's acorns with his children a year before and now had some eight seedlings that in another five or six hundred years might grow to rival the parent tree. A local foundry operator had put forth the idea to cast the tree in bronze, so that in years to come a full-size statue would mark the spot where Treaty Oak lived and died. And there were other memorial acts planned: The Men's Garden Club of Austin would take cuttings from the dying tree, and corporate sponsors were being sought out to pay for an expensive tissue culture that would ensure genetically identical Treaty Oak clones.

"I hope you live so I can bring my children to see you," read a note left at the tree by J. J. Albright, of La Grange, Texas, age nine. There were innumerable others like it— from other children, from grownups, from bankers, from pagans and Baptists, all of them talking to the tree, all of them wanting in some way to lay their hands upon its dying tissue and heal it. Perhaps this was all nonsense and I had just been living in Austin too long to realize it or admit it to myself. But I was enough of a pagan to believe that all the weirdness was warranted, that Treaty Oak had some message to deliver, and that no one could predict through which channel it would ultimately be received.

My own sad premonition was that the tree would die, though not in the way Sharon Capehart had predicted, in an ascending glory of light. I felt that at some point in the months to come its animate essence would quietly slip away. But for now it was still an unyielding entity, mysteriously alive and demanding, still rooted defiantly to the earth.

Standing there, feeling attuned to the tree's power and to the specter of its death, I recalled with a shudder a ghastly incident I had not thought of in years. When I was in college, a young woman I knew slightly had burned herself to death at the foot of Treaty Oak. I remembered her as bright and funny, carelessly good-looking. But one day she had walked to the tree, poured gasoline all over her body, and struck a match.

The newspaper report said that a neighbor had heard her moan and rushed to her rescue with a half-gallon wine bottle filled with water. By the time he got there she was no longer on fire, but her hair and clothes were burned away and she was in shock, stunned beyond pain. Waiting for the ambulance, they carried on a conversation. She asked the man to kill her. He of course refused, and when he asked her why she had done this to herself, she would not respond. But why here? he wanted to know. Why do it here at the Treaty Oak? For that she had an answer.

"Because," she said, "it's a nice place to be."

Highway One

It had been raining hard for a week, and on this still overcast day the country beyond Loop 1604 was lush with suppressed light. Here, on the frontier of San Antonio's suburban expansion, the land retained a suggestion of primeval Texas. Blazing swaths of wildflowers had taken over the brushy landscape, and in the creek bottoms the stout hardwoods were knitted together with tensile loops of vine.

The particular tree I was looking for, an aged live oak, stood by itself on the edge of the road in a field of white poppies. In the center of its trunk was the scar of an old wound, so smoothed and weathered by time that now it appeared only as a faint gray stain in the bark. Had I not been looking for it, I would not have recognized it for what it was, would not have seen that the wound was in the shape of a cross.

Someone had carved the cross into this tree hundreds of years ago, probably a Franciscan priest accompanying one of the many Spanish expeditions that made their way through Texas up the Camino Real, the "Royal Road" or King's Highway that ran from San Juan Bautista on the Rio Grande to the failing missions scattered west of the Sabine. At one time, along the various ragged trails that made up the Camino Real, there must have been many crosses like this one marking the way, signs to invoke the presence of God in the wilderness, tokens of thanksgiving for a safe river crossing or the passing of a furious storm.

Today only a few are left, and where you find them you find the road.

In front of this tree I could make out an eroded vestige of the Camino Real, a shallow, meandering rift in the ground that looked no more imposing than a creek drainage. And yet this barely perceptible ditch was once the track upon which New Spain made its fitful, conquering advance into the wilderness beyond the Rio Grande. It was the basic route along which the history of Texas would be determined. Though many of the missions and presidios that the Spaniards established along the Camino Real rotted away in the jungle humidity of the East Texas forests, others took root and grew into cities like Nacogdoches and San Antonio. As early as Spanish Colonial times, the road served as a boundary to mark land grants. It was used by French smugglers and by Anglo-American filibusters. The Camino Real was the road that both Davy Crockett and Santa Anna—coming from different directions—traveled to reach the Alamo.

No one knows precisely how long the road has existed. Before it was a Spanish thoroughfare it was probably an Indian trail, and the Indian trail itself may have followed a route first defined by the hooves of migrating bison. According to the Texas Legislature, which enacted a Senate resolution to commemorate the road, the Camino Real would be three hundred years old in 1991. "The roadway," reads the resolution, "was officially established under the authority of the first provincial governor of Texas under Spanish rule in 1691."

Since history records no ribbon-cutting or other ceremony to mark the official inauguration of the Camino Real, however, the Legislature's announcement of a 300th anniversary is a bit arbitrary. The provincial governor referred to in the resolution—a man named Terán de los Ríos—did use the road in 1691 to travel into the interior of Texas, but the route of the Camino Real had already been laid out during the course of two previous expeditions led by Alonso de León. Almost everything having to do with the Camino Real—its origins, its exact course, even its name—is hazy and half defined. In the days when Texas was a part of Spain, "Camino Real" referred to an official highway, a road—however rough—that linked the king's holdings and helped to further imperial policy. On the King's Highway, you traveled under the king's protection.

The Camino Real that crossed Texas is better known as the Old San Antonio Road, and that is how the Legislature refers to it in its anniversary resolution. As a name, "Old San Antonio Road" is a holdover from the nineteenth century. When the Camino Real was first blazed in the late seventeenth century, San Antonio did not yet exist. The original orientation of the road was toward the east, from the Rio Grande to the Sabine, and on into Louisiana. Later, as the Spanish hold on Texas grew shaky, settlers and provocateurs from the United States streamed down the road from the opposite direction.

Finding exactly where the road ran—from either direction—is a complicated business. Though traces of the Camino Real are still visible here and there, for much of its length the road is a ghost, grown over or paved under, disappearing between the established reference points. Its presence can only be inferred. In 1915 the Texas Legislature hired a civil engineer named V. N. Zivley to locate the road and mark it. Zivley threw himself into the task with antique patriotic fervor. "This is the road," he wrote, "over and by which most of those 'mighty men of valor' who afterwards founded and established the Republic of Texas, unfurling the Lone Star Flag to the balmy Southern breezes, entered the land of their choice."

Zivley had no great trouble locating the basic route of the "Anglo" section of the Camino Real, the part that ran from east to west. The route Zivley marked follows the course of Texas Highway 21, through San Augustine, Nacogdoches, Alto, Crockett, and Bastrop and into San Antonio—"the City of the Alamo" the engineer noted, "that altar consecrated by Anglo-Saxon blood to the God of Liberty."

South of San Antonio, Zivley found the road considerably more difficult to trace. The physical evidence was faint and spotty, and about the only thing Zivley could find to document the course of the road was a diary kept by a priest named Juan Agustín Morfi in 1778 ("to that old padre," a relieved Zivley wrote, "though I am Protestant of the most ultra blue stocking type, I want to doff my hat").

Zivley's reckoning of the route was accurate enough for its time, taking into account his obvious bias toward that part of the road upon which Anglo-Saxon feet had trod. A few years after his survey, the Daughters of the American Revolution commemorated the route he designated by erecting hundreds of pink-granite markers, one every five miles. The markers were scrupulously placed along the actual route that Zivley marked, but since in many instances this was an out-of-the-way spot, citizens dug them up and moved them to more prominent locations like courthouse lawns or highway rest stops (in some counties, every single marker has been displaced). And over the decades, as more and more archival records from the Spanish Colonial period have come to light, Zivley's confident accounting of the road's course has become less and less definitive.

For the 300th anniversary of the Camino Real, the Legislature directed the Texas Department of Highways and Public Transportation to, in essence, find the road again. The highway department and the Texas Historical Commission were to present a historic preservation plan to the Legislature. They had a year to do this and a staff of five. When I dropped in at their Austin office, one day in April, they were about halfway through.

"It's a booger," Al McGraw, the staff archaeologist and project director, told me. He was smoking a pipe in a windowless storage room, whose long rows of shelves held various archaeological artifacts. In other rooms the staff was poring over photocopies of old land grants, deeds, historic maps, and survey reports. One entire wall was covered with a chart that broke down the details of each of the Spanish expedition diaries: date, starting and ending locations, leagues traveled (a Spanish league is 2.6 miles), direction, and comments ("passed the point of a little hill where oak clump ends at 1/2 league from camp"; "crossed 2 creeks; pecan and oak woods for 5 leagues"). Out of such puzzle pieces a coherent picture of the road was slowly emerging.

But the clearer the date, the more fragmentary and various the Camino Real became. The essential road of Texas history, McGraw and his staff were discovering, was not, strictly speaking, one road at all. "What you have to realize," McGraw said, pointing to a Texas map that had a series of interwoven lines drawn on it in different colored markers, "is that the Camino Real—the Old San Antonio Road, whatever you want to call it— was not just a single trail. It was a network."

The lines on the map reminded me of an erratic riverbed, constantly meandering and shifting, a series of braided channels that ultimately led to the same destination. Each variant of the braid had its own name: the Upper Presidio Road, the Lower Presidio Road, the Camino Pita, the Camino de los Tejas, the Camino Arriba. The reason for this web of routes is easy to understand. In its early existence the road was a faint track, hardly more than a suggestion. Almost every expedition that used it found a way to improve upon it. Over time the travelers discovered more-efficient river crossings or routes that would help them skirt natural obstacles such as El Atascosa, the boggy alluvial plain south of San Antonio, or the dense forest—El Monte— near present-day Bastrop, under whose gloomy canopy the Spanish soldiers tended to grow anxious and disoriented. It is believed that when the Apaches, pressured by the Comanches to the north, began to raid below the Hill Country, the road looped south into the less hospitable brush land to avoid them.

But all the routes began in the same place, at a frontier outpost known as San Juan Bautista that sat in a pecan glade on the south bank of the Rio Grande. At the time the Camino Real was created, San Juan Bautista was nothing more than a remote settlement built around a mission and the presidio that guarded it. Over time, however, it became a major staging area for the royal expeditions that filtered up to the unknown lands of Texas.

The town that grew up around San Juan Bautista is called Guererro and is enthrallingly old. I drove there one day in late spring, crossing the border at Eagle Pass, driving through Piedras Negras, and heading about thirty miles east into the Mexican state of Coahuila. In mid-afternoon, the streets and square of Guererro were empty, and the town had the echoing stillness of a stopped clock. There were no sounds except those that might have been heard here three hundred years ago—the creaky calls of Chihuahuan ravens, the crowing of roosters, the noise of the wind rushing through the pecan leaves overhead.

The parade ground of the old presidio had become the town square, and many of the ancient buildings from Spanish Colonial times—the presidio captain's house, the paymaster's house—were not only still standing but still in use. Some of the houses now had modern stucco fronts, but along their sides I could see the bare walls of stacked stone, the mortar long since eroded away.

Other structures were vacant and half fallen in. I chose one and walked inside. Most of the roof had collapsed, and the floor was a weedy mass of rubble and broken bottles. The house had been unused for so long that a large tree had grown inside of it, though in an adjoining room the old roof beams were still in place, supporting a few remaining scraps of brittle sod over-grown with prickly pear.

Emerging through a low doorway, I stood for a moment in the sun and gazed across the square, at the former *plaza de armas* of the presidio. The occupants of this house might have stood in this same spot, watching the various *entradas* assemble and march off in high spirits toward the Rio Grande, the first of the many rivers they would cross in their journey through what is now the state of Texas.

Those early expeditions crossed the Rio Grande at a place several miles distant, called Paso Francia—"Frenchman's Crossing." It was called that for a reason. Near the end of the seventeenth century, Spain's claim that it possessed the land beyond the Rio Grande was not much more than rhetoric. In fact, the march of Spanish civilization had just about stalled out in the deserts of northern Mexico. Texas was a looming wilderness at the farthest margin of Spain's farthest frontier. There was no compelling reason to venture into it, and hence no need for a royal road.

But the Spaniards were roused to action when they heard rumors that the French had invaded Texas from the Gulf of Mexico and had planted a colony somewhere on the coast. These rumors were given alarming credence in 1688, when Alonso de León, the governor of Coahuila, happened upon a Frenchman living in an Indian village about sixty miles north of the Rio Grande, west of present-day Uvalde. The man was about fifty years old and crazy, but he had managed to entice the Indians into treating him like a potentate. De León found him sitting on a cushion made of buffalo hide while members of his court cooled him with feather fans. He was surrounded by a bodyguard of forty warriors.

When he saw his visitors, he jumped up from the cushion, pumped their hands in greeting, kissed the priest's scapular, and happily announced in his fractured Spanish, "Yo *frances!* (I French!)"

"I am going about assembling many Indian nations," he told De León, "to make them my friends; those who do not wish to join me, I attack and destroy with the aid of my Indian followers."

Exactly who he was, what he was up to, and where he had come from nobody ever really knew—least of all the befuddled Frenchman himself. But something he told De León helped change the course of history. He said that a French settlement—with a fort and a township—had been established on the banks of a "large river to the east" and had been there for fifteen years.

There was indeed a French fort. De León spent the next year looking for it and in the process opened up the route of the Camino Real. But instead of a formidable French presence, he found only a ruined and looted stockade, the ground strewn with pig carcasses, rotting books in leather bindings, and a woman's skeleton still wearing the tattered scraps of a dress. That was all that was left of Fort St. Louis, the colony that the French explorer Sieur de la Salle had attempted to establish on Matagorda Bay. La Salle himself had been killed by his own men, and the rest of the desperate colonists had been overrun by Karankawas.

The French threat seemed to have taken care of itself,

but because of it the Spanish road into Texas had been opened, and De León's next discovery helped guarantee that it would remain so. Traveling north and east, pursuing rumors of French survivors, he entered the country of the Hasinai, a confederation of tribes whose name in all its variations—Tayshas, Taychas, Tehas, Teias, Texia, Teisa, Teyans, Tejas—meant "friend." De León found the "kingdom of the Texas," and it indeed seemed to be a land of friendship and welcome. These Caddoan people were settled and affluent—skilled farmers who kept their surplus maize and beans in watertight cribs inside their huge conical houses. To the Spaniards' astonishment, they had even been visited by the Woman in Blue.

The Woman in Blue was a weird spiritual phenomenon of seventeenth-century Spain. In physical reality, she was a Castilian abbess named Mother María de Jesús de Agreda. María de Agreda never left her convent in Spain—but she became famous for her claims that she was able to transport herself to faraway Texas. There she appeared before the Indians as a beautiful woman in a blue cloak, bewitching them into Christian belief.

So far, the Woman in Blue had shown herself only to the Indians living along the Rio Grande, but now here was evidence that her spirit was roving deep into the unknown lands to the east. It is reported that the Hasinai chief whom De León encountered even had a portable altar, complete with figures of Christ and the saints, in front of which a light was kept burning in perpetual veneration. The chief told Father Damian Massanet, the priest accompanying De León, that he would welcome further spiritual instruction.

So all at once New Spain had compelling business in distant Texas. It would establish presidios to guard its borders against the French and missions to turn the Indians into servants of God and Spain. To do all this, it would need a road.

The road came into being slowly, league by league, river crossing by river crossing. It was never actually "built" but simply improved upon, its route modified by almost every expedition that used it. To call it a road at all is misleading. The Camino Real was not nearly as imposing, for instance, as the broad curbed highways the Anasazi Indians had built hundreds of years before, far to the west in the New Mexican desert. The Spanish road was a track, rarely wider than a single oxcart, and often so indecipherable that the professional explorers who followed it routinely got lost.

When I left Guererro, traveling northeast toward San Antonio, I was following the general trend of the Camino Real, but there was hardly any physical evidence to mark the actual route of the old road. I crossed the Nueces, the Hondo, the Medina, glancing down at the rivers from the highway bridges as I sped across, thinking of the Spanish horses churning madly in the water, and the soldiers and Indians ferrying sheep across one at a time.

The crossings were routinely hazardous. On Domingo Ramón's 1716 expedition, eighty-two horses were drowned trying to reach the far bank of the Medina. Ramón, sensing the devil's hand in this calamity, ordered a mass the next day "to crush him." Don Domingo de Terán, starting out on the first expedition to establish the missions in East Texas, lost forty-nine saddle horses to the Rio Grande. "However, the great power of Our Lady of Guadalupe, the North Star and protector of this undertaking, carried our weak efforts in this task to a successful ending."

Day by day these *entradas* had staggered down the rude path of the Camino Real—the soldiers outfitted in buckskin or quilted cotton, plodding along under the weight of their harquebuses and leather shields; the friars and lay brothers in their brown robes, a few of them heroically barefoot, the rest with their gnarled and swollen feet encased in sandals; the mission Indians driving herds of goats and sheep; the oxcarts packed with trading goods and religious implements, including holy-water fonts and ovens for baking communion wafers; and the banners overhead, bearing the images of Our Lady of Pilar or Our Lady of Guadalupe or Saint James the Moor-Killer.

When I reached San Antonio, I traveled along Mission Road, more or less following the course of the old road as it passed icehouses and auto-repair shops and Pig Stands, almost incidentally passing the missions of San Juan Capistrano, San Francisco de la Espada, San José and Nuestra Señora de la Purísima Concepción. These missions were begun by the Spaniards early in the eighteenth century, after those in East Texas had been abandoned and the padres were ordered to retrench along the San Antonio River, where the local Indians proved to be ultimately more agreeable than the Hasinai.

Domingo Ramón's expedition of 1716 had been the first to describe San Antonio Springs, the glorious headwaters of the San Antonio River. It was near there, two years later, that the village of San Antonio de Béxar was founded. The first mission to be built in the town—San Antonio de Valero—was moved twice, allowed to fall into ruin, and finally secularized in 1793. For a time it served as the headquarters for a Spanish cavalry from a town in Mexico named Alamo de las Parras.

I parked my car in a lot by the San Antonio River and

walked through the lobby of the Hyatt Hotel to Alamo Plaza. Standing in front of the chapel, I reckoned that the Camino Real would have passed a few hundred yards to the east, and I tried to imagine Santa Anna's forces wheeling into position for the siege. Striking out in 1836 from Mexico to suppress the rebellion in Texas, Santa Anna had driven his army up the road in a cold-blooded forced march that left many of them buried along the way, his bewildered conscripts from the tropical jungles of the Yucatán dropping from exposure in a freak blizzard.

And this is where the Camino Real had led him. The Battle of the Alamo was no accident. By 1836 Anglo-American immigrants had for several decades been on a collision course with the Spanish and Mexican governments that held Texas, and now the two cultures hurtled toward each other from opposite ends of the Camino Real like locomotives on a single track. The wreck had to occur someplace, and that someplace—sitting smack in the middle of the road—was the Alamo.

Leaving San Antonio, I took Interstate 35 north, which kept me roughly parallel to the route of the old Camino. Near San Marcos, I met up with Stephen L. Hardin, a historian working for the highway department on the Old San Antonio Road project. Tall and bearded, Hardin wore a cap featuring the logo of the Sons of the Republic of Texas and a belt buckle emblazoned with the state seal. For the last four months, he and fellow researchers had been reading and annotating old diaries, searching for maps and land records, interviewing farmers and ranchers, and driving from one end of Texas to the other, trying to uncover archival or physical clues that would pinpoint the road.

"John Ford movies to the contrary," he told me as we

drove along in his beat-up Subaru, "a bunch of guys just can't head off across the prairie. You've got to have a road. And it's axiomatic that roads follow roads, that new paths follow old paths when they're able to. For instance, I-35—from about York Creek south to San Antonio—is the lower Camino. This road we're on now"—we were driving on a dirt road off 183, the Lockhart Highway—"follows the original route of the later Camino Real. And I think it made an arc down here and linked up with Highway 21. If you'd been a volunteer coming down from Louisiana to fight in the Texas Revolution, this is the road you would have taken up to the Alamo.

"Now, I've been told," Hardin said, stopping the car a few miles east of San Marcos, near the intersection of Highway 80 and Highway 21, "that you can see swales of the Camino Real on this golf course."

He got out to look, squinting and studying the contours of the fairways as golfers teed off under the trees, but he could find no marks of the old road. A few miles further south, though, on the Old Bastrop Road, he pulled over and pointed to a deep ditch on the other side of the barbed-wire fence.

"In terms of physical evidence," Hardin said, climbing onto the fragile roof of the Subaru for a better view, "this is one of the best places in Texas to see the road."

It looked nothing like a road, of course. One of the unexpected peculiarities of the Camino Real is that it is preserved not just in shallow ruts but in pronounced gullies, because centuries of rain have channeled water into the original roadbed and scoured it deeper. The gully here was grown over with bluebonnets. It ran straight for several hundred yards and then, near the crest of a shallow hill, curved and closed up like a seam.

We spent the rest of the afternoon in San Marcos, where Hardin pondered the question of exactly where Domingo Ramón's expedition would have crossed the river in 1716. Hardin had established that the Camino Real came in from the west, following the course of present-day Hopkins Street, but he doubted that Ramón had crossed the river where the Hopkins Street bridge now stood. The water was too deep there, the bottom too sandy, the banks too steep.

"Espinosa provides the best clue," Hardin said. (Espinosa was a priest and diarist of the Ramón expedition.) "He says that they crossed the San Marcos two harquebus shots from the headwaters. A harquebus shot is not usually more than a hundred yards."

That brought us to the Sewell Park bridge, just below the tourist attraction of Aquarena Springs. Here the banks of the river were lower, and through the clear, shallow water we could see the gravelly bottom.

"This is all becoming clear to me," Hardin said, growing excited. "They probably came in on Hopkins Street, found it a bad place to cross, then followed the bank upstream a little ways.

"It's obvious," he said, pounding the steering wheel with his fist as we drove past the entrance to Aquarena Springs. Above us, on the left, the Balcones Escarpment rose in stark perspective. "It's obvious what they did! After they crossed the river they would have followed the hills! It becomes clear now. It becomes clear! This is the perfect place for a road. You know, sometimes it just bites you on the butt!"

After I parted company with Hardin, I drove east, through Bastrop, following the ghostly route of the Camino Real as best I could along Highway 21 as it led from the edge of the Hill Country to pastoral prairies and logged-over forests replaced with a roadside veneer of pines. This was the section of the road over which Zivley's "mighty men of valor" had come tromping into Texas, and the success of this Anglo-Saxon thoroughfare was memorialized in the very asphalt under my tires. That this was the Old San Antonio Road was proudly proclaimed by highway signs and by the pink-granite markers of 1918 along the roadside. In Crockett, at the bottom of a railroad overpass next to a gas station, I noticed a billboard-size sign proclaiming "The David Crockett Spring." The sign depicted Crockett drinking from a gurgling pool as deer, rabbits, and armadillos respectfully looked on. "The David Crockett Spring," the sign read, "Which marks the camp site of the famous Texan [never mind that he was a Tennessean!] on his historic journey to the Alamo where he paid the supreme price for Texas Liberty."

Farther down the road, outside of Alto, I stopped at the roadside grave of Helena Kimbell Dill Nelson— "Mother of Child thought to have been first Anglo-American born in Texas, in 1804." The vault had been reinterred in concrete, and the lettering on the tablet was so eroded that it looked as if it had been carved in salt instead of marble. But the fact that this simple grave had become a monument only emphasized the central irony of the Camino Real. The road that the Spanish had originally blazed to ensure that no foreigners could penetrate their borders had in the end become an avenue of conquest.

Highway 21 led into Nacogdoches, where it became a red-brick street running through the center of town. Main Street had, indisputably, grown up on the exact course of the Camino Real. There was no need to look for river crossings or swales to infer the presence of the road.

This was it, still in use, still the main street of this ancient city. Nacogdoches began as a Hasinai village, and just a block from downtown I located a stunted burial mound, covered with grass, standing by the curb in somebody's front yard with such matter-of-factness that my initial reaction was to wonder how difficult it was to mow.

Nacogdoches' strategic location exposed it over the years to every wind that swept down the Camino Real—from those first Spanish expeditions to roust the French and establish missions to the half-dozen attempts by Anglo-Americans to pry Texas away from Spain and Mexico.

Adolphus Sterne, a Nacogdoches merchant, was one of the principal financiers of the definitive Anglo uprising, the Texas Revolution of 1836. When sentiment against Mexican authority was at its highest, Sterne traveled to New Orleans and raised a company of volunteers he called the New Orleans Greys. Sterne outfitted the Greys with surplus muskets and uniforms he had found in an armory building on Magazine Street—gray fatigue jackets, white belts, wooden canteens, and U.S. Army forage caps made out of sealskin.

The Greys were doomed. Few of them would survive the revolution. But they came marching into Texas on the Camino Real in fine spirits, toasted as heroes and saviors by the settlers along the way. Among them was a German youth named Herman Ehrenberg, who later recalled the banquet that Adolphus Sterne gave the Greys in a field in front of his house.

Adolphus Sterne's house still stands in Nacogdoches, just a few yards off the Camino Real. And in front of it is the field where that long-ago fandango was held. The main course at dinner, Ehrenberg remembered vividly, was a roasted bear named Mr. Petz.

"This huge creature," Ehrenberg wrote, "was so skillfully dressed in his fur that he seemed to be still alive; his mouth was drawn back in a fierce grin and showed sharp, white teeth tightly holding the true colors of the 1824 constitution. Raccoons, opossums, squirrels, and monkeys surrounded Mr. Petz, while two large legs of mutton, roasted to a nice brown, and a substantial joint of beef completed the decoration of our board."

From Nacogdoches most of the Greys went on to fight and die at the Alamo or be executed at Goliad. Herman Ehrenberg was one of only a handful of men to survive the Goliad massacre. Reeling from a sword wound to the head, blinded by gunpowder, he jumped into the river shouting—he would have us believe—"The Republic of Texas forever!" and managed, after many other adventures, to find his way back to the Texas army. After that he went home to Germany and wrote his memoirs to pay his way through college.

From Nacogdoches I headed east, stopping in San Augustine at the site of Mission Nuestra Señora Dolores de los Ais, founded by Father Antonio Margil de Jesús in 1716. Fray Margil was the most venerated character ever to set foot on the Camino Real—a restless, dauntless, almost pathologically holy man who slept three hours a night, hardly ever ate, and was so humble he signed all his correspondence *La Misma Nada*, "The Same as Nothing."

Margil was born in Valencia, Spain. His favorite activity as a child was building miniature altars, and when he began studying for the priesthood, he mortified his flesh with such enthusiasm that the Master of Novices, alarmed, took away his hair shirt.

Arriving as a missionary in the New World, he threw away his sandals and impressed the Indians by sometimes wearing a crown of thorns and trudging around under the weight of a heavy cross. He wandered barefoot through all the wild lands of Central America, establishing missions and apostolic colleges and narrowly escaping, time and again, the martyrdom he craved. He became so famous that sometimes when he approached a village he would find an arch erected in his honor and hundreds of people waiting to strew flowers in his path. This of course horrified him. He wanted only the ecstasy of oblivion. On his deathbed, he maintained that he did not even deserve a Christian burial, that he should instead be tossed "out in the wilds, where the beasts can devour me." The priest who heard his last, brief confession was of the opinion that he had never lost his "baptismal innocence."

But not even Margil could make the East Texas missions a successful enterprise. They were a disaster almost from the beginning. The Hasinai might have been originally entranced by this exotic new religion, but they were such accomplished farmers that the idea of abandoning their fields to plant mission crops made no sense. In some areas, smallpox killed half the Hasinai population. The priests mobilized to baptize the dying, but as the Indians watched the holy men pour water over the victims' heads, they concluded that the act of baptism itself was lethal. Nor did they care for the lamb broth that the priests fed the sick. They called it "dirty water."

Mission Dolores de las Ais was abandoned in 1719, its wooden church and buildings slowly disintegrating in the humid air. Now there is nothing left of it, except for a few pottery shards and ancient post holes found by archaeologists and the historical marker sitting on an overgrown bluff above a stream terrace.

At Milam, on the Texas side of the Sabine, I turned off to call on Earl and Ingrid Morris. Earl is a local building contractor whose ancestor, Shadrack Morris, founded Sabine Town, a once-thriving settlement along the river. His wife, Ingrid, had been appointed by the governor to serve on the Texas Preservation Commission. One of her areas of concern was how to commemorate the road once its route had been established.

The Morrises had offered to show me a cabin built in 1819 or so by James Gaines, who operated the ferry on the Sabine that the New Orleans Greys had used to cross into Texas. "At one time there were two thousand people here," Ingrid said as we drove through the highway junction of Milam. "They even had a permanent gallows."

She pointed to what looked like a bar ditch near the side of the road. "See that groove behind that old truck? That's the Camino Real. It passed right behind that tree line, into the old town square."

"This particular place here," Earl said, when we had traveled a few miles farther, "the road probably went around. It may not be real boggy around here, but there are sloughs all in it. Not really swamps, but pin-oak ponds and baygalls. Back then you would have wanted to go above your boggy places. If you've got a wide cart with big round wheels and an ox pulling it, you might make it through the donkey grass, but if you've got a narrow-wheeled wagon loaded down with pianos, it's a different story."

The cabin stood in a forested subdivision, set off by itself on its original site near a hollow sweet gum tree that Earl said was the home of a family of bobcats. The cabin was grander and stouter than I had expected, a one-and-a-half-story structure with dogtrots on both floors, made of sturdy logs of square-notched longleaf pine. Light shone through the gaps between the logs where the batting had been removed for restoration, but the house was solid.

"It's a very well-trimmed-out house for the time," Earl said as we stepped inside. "And the floor's all hand-planed." He squatted down and rubbed his palm across the floorboards. "Whoever planed this was very good. It's so discreet. You can't feel the grain."

It was a haunting place, haunting in its solidity, in the way it made the world of the Camino Real so suddenly vivid and timeless. Upstairs, on one of the walls, was a reminder about a steamboat departure—"the Buffalo will leave Hamilton for the pass Thursday at 4"—written in chalk 150 years ago.

When we left the cabin we strolled into the woods that fringed the clearing, leaving the bright sunlight for the deep, brambly shade. When we had walked only a few yards, Earl turned to me and announced, "We're standing right on it."

We were in a narrow groove half filled with leaves: the Camino Real. To the left the groove continued toward the river and the now-submerged site of Gaines's ferry. Beyond that was Louisiana. If it had been three hundred years ago, I could have turned to my right and started walking, keeping a sharp eye out for the trail, and ended up a few months later in San Juan Bautista.

But it would be impossible to follow the road now, and no point to it unless you were one of those people who feel complete only when face to face with the vestiges and traces of a vanished world they can never know. As we stood there in the roadbed, odd little bits of lore from those Camino Real diaries kept floating into my mind: the mules neglecting the coarse pasturage along the road to eat the moss off the trees; the sudden windstorm that picked up a horse and rider and deposited them several yards away; the small boy who wandered away from camp and was never found; the Hasinai priest who had put out his own eyes in order to enhance his spiritual sight.

Parts of the old Camino Real—like Highway 21—are still in business, but the days when it was the great Texas road are long gone. After Texas won its independence from Mexico in 1836, the Camino Real quickly began to lose its significance. The new republic looked east to the United States, not south to its old enemy. There was no great need for a road to the Rio Grande when goods were streaming in from St. Louis and New Orleans. In this new Texas, the Camino Real led nowhere. By 1850, ranchers were asking for—and receiving—permission to string fences across it.

Yet here it was, still etched in this trough of soft dirt—a bygone route of imperial conquest, where people had once walked under the official protection of the King of Spain. Near where we stood I noticed a collapsed earthen bank, littered with rotten timber and overgrown with vines.

"You know what that is?" Earl asked. "Back in the early sixties somebody scooped some dirt out of the road here and built himself an atomic-bomb shelter."

He smiled and kicked gently at the dirt with his feet. "You see," he said, "there's uses for the old Camino Real yet."

The Bay

The wind is light, an idle spring breeze, but it gusts forcefully across the bay, turning the water's surface into a field of percolating whitecaps. A short distance from shore, an unladen tanker coasts through the chop, heading up past Morgan's Point to Buffalo Bayou and the Port of Houston. Its wake loses definition among the unruly wave patterns and ends up as a tired riffle that washes against the eroded shoreline—against piers and bulkheads and stretches of protective riprap formed from old car bodies and pieces of concrete culvert. There is a vague, watermelon-like scent in the air—the smell of fish oil and fish blood released from the bodies of shad or mullet as they are torn apart by predators that have herded them into a roiling, panicky mass. On the edge of the Ship Channel a shrimp boat, winching in its nets, is almost obscured by a cloud of laughing gulls. The gulls are in their breeding colors, their bright red beaks shining like enamel in the clear air.

Galveston Bay can sometimes appear picturesque; it could not be truthfully described as beautiful. Its waters are shallow and murky, an opaque green marbled with currents of resuspended mud left behind by the passage of boats and pipeline dredges. Its shorelines are drab and abrupt. Much of the western margin of the bay is dominated by a petrochemical skyline, a hazy gridwork of twisting pipelines and flaming towers. Nowhere else is there such a concentrated display of the raw wealth that built Texas or of the price the natural environment has paid for that wealth. The bay has been despoiled for so long, has been used so hard, that it has developed a perverse allure. Ross Sterling, the governor of Texas from 1931 to 1933, once built a scaled-down replica of the White House for himself near La Porte. The view he most admired from the roof terrace of his dream home was the lights of the refineries on the opposite shore.

Galveston Bay is a working bay. Take away the shipping, the refining, the whole thrumming human presence, and there is still a feel of industry about it. The bay is a mighty thing, a self-adjusting biological engine that runs day and night, season after season, constantly generating and absorbing life. It is the largest estuary on the Texas coast, the seventh largest in the United States, a vast nursery and feedlot where all manner of marine larvae, spats, and fingerlings pass their perilous youths. Even the people most concerned about preserving the bay have grown accustomed to speaking of it in terms of its productivity, as a resource, as if in order to justify its existence it must compete with the commerce surrounding it. At a time in which the salvation of the oceans has suddenly appeared as one of the planet's highest priorities, Texas still thinks of its poisoned waters with a sense of dollars lost instead of a sense of shame.

On maps, the bay has the shape of a mashed butterfly. One wing is made up of a gracefully curving shoreline that includes the entrance to the Houston Ship Channel on the west and the Trinity River delta on the east. The other wing, flattened and truncated, is known as East Bay and runs east behind the Bolivar Peninsula. Trailing the butterfly is a long, narrow tendril—called West Bay—that makes up the inward shore of Galveston Island. It all amounts to six hundred square miles of water sitting in a shallow basin of mud. Fresh water enters the bay from the San Jacinto River and, to a much greater extent, from the Trinity, whose drainage area pulls rainwater and runoff into the bay from as far away as Fort Worth. From the sea, the saltwater tide flows in through the mile-wide gap where Galveston Island and Bolivar Peninsula fail to meet, a narrow but vital thoroughfare known as Bolivar Roads.

   This mixture of salt water and fresh water in the bay is a hospitable one. It gives rise to an almost inconceivable abundance of life, millions and millions of pounds of harvested sea creatures, flapping and scuttling about on the decks of sport boats and commercial vessels. The catch is so abundant that oysters and crabs from Galveston Bay are eaten on the shores of the Chesapeake Bay.

   But the bay is decidedly not what it once was. John James Audubon came to Galveston Bay in 1837, when Texas was still so new a republic that one of the few things a tourist could buy was a Mexican skull picked up off the battlefield of San Jacinto. Audubon was not in the best of moods on this trip. He had lost twelve pounds, his legs were swollen, and the mosquitoes, he wrote, "were annoying enough even for me." But his mind was as engaged as ever. He took note of the birds that had been forced down in their northern migrations by a powerful storm, reported finding a new species of rattlesnake, and discovered a large swordfish stranded on a sandbar that, when cut open, produced ten wriggling young.

The abundance and beauty of the bay seemed to revive him. "Ah, my dear friend," Audubon wrote in a letter, "would that you were here just now to see the Snipes innumerable, the Blackbirds, the Gallinules, and the Curlews that surround us;—that you could listen as I now do, to the delightful notes of the Mocking-bird, pouring forth his soul in melody as the glorious orb of day is fast descending towards the western horizon;— that you could gaze on the Great Herons which, after spreading their broad wings, croak aloud as if doubtful regarding the purpose of our visit to these shores!"

If it was the Eskimo curlew that Audubon was refer-ring to in his letter, that bird is now almost extinct. It was once one of the most abundant shorebirds on Galveston Bay. Eskimo curlews were called doughbirds because the thick, fatty meat of their breasts was as pale and soft as dough. They were killed by the hundreds of thousands— their plump breasts splitting open when they hit the ground—packed in barrels, and sent back east. The last one seen in the vicinity was spotted on Galveston Island in the early sixties.

The bottom of the bay, in Audubon's time, was carpeted with seagrass meadows, great swaths of turtle grass and eelgrass that fixed the sediment and kept the water clear. He would have seen stands of primeval cypress where there are now container docks; expanses of shortgrass prairie, with vultures nesting in the prickly pear, where there are now coastal bermuda and asphalt. He might have seen manatees idling below the surface, as smooth and slow as dirigibles.

All of that is gone, all but the bay itself. If it is no longer the wonder that filled Audubon's heart, it remains a marvel of resilience. How could it even still exist, after all the life that has been extracted from it, all the chemicals and wastewater sludge and brine that have been pumped into it, all the development that has taken place on its shores? More than half of the chemicals produced in the United States come from the area around Galveston Bay. Thirty percent of the nation's petroleum industry is located there. Twenty percent of the people who live in Texas live somewhere along the bay's margin. Municipal and industrial wastewater is discharged into the bay from 1,151 registered treatment plants. Beneath the surface are 251 miles of dredged channels, 247 miles of pipeline. The water contains DDT, aliphatic hydrocarbons, aromatic hydrocarbons, organophosphates. There is chromium, copper, lead, nickel, zinc, and mercury. Fifty-one percent of the bay is permanently closed to shellfish harvesting because of bacterial pollution. Ninety-five percent of the seagrass has disappeared. Bulkheads and marinas are replacing the cordgrass marshes that incubate marine life and prevent erosion. Poachers are collecting and eating the eggs from the few scraggly islands where shorebirds still find it congenial to nest. And there are two looming projects—the deepening and widening of the Houston Ship Channel and the completion of the Wallisville Reservoir near the mouth of the Trinity—which some environmentalists believe could seal the fate of the bay.

"Your article may be an epitaph," Ted Eubanks, the president of the Houston Audubon Society, told me one day as we stood on the hypnotic expanse of Bolivar Flats, observing piping plovers through a spotting scope. "The destruction of Galveston Bay is running full speed."

Eubanks, who owns a trucking business in Houston, delivered this dire prophecy with his usual air of ominous reason. I recognized his opinion as being on the alarmist end of the scale, a surly, brokenhearted lament of the sort that I had heard dismissed, more than once, as "emotional." But in the long history of human abuse of the bay, emotion has been a conspicuously absent quality. Galveston Bay was always there to be exploited—its original beauty so subtle as to be hardly noticed during the raucous coming-out party of the Texas economy.

Optimists argue that twenty years ago the bay was in much worse shape. The nearly unimpeded dumping of municipal and industrial waste in the Houston Ship Channel had turned the water into an oxygen-depleted witch's brew of toxic compounds and sewer sludge— "the only ship channel in the world," Lloyd Bentsen has quipped, "to have an octane rating." The Ship Channel is still far away from being a swimmable and fishable stream, but the passage of the Clean Water Act in 1970 and a growing environmental awareness helped curb the blithe excesses of industry. The Houston Ship Channel currently has a dissolved oxygen rating of one, a step up from the anaerobic zero it used to be but far from the five required for "contact-recreation." ("Fish can live in category-one water," an employee of the Texas Water

Commission told me, "they just can't scoot around much.") And after decades of dreadful wastewater problems, the City of Houston has finally entered into a compliance agreement with the water commission that, ten years and $1 billion from now, will have reduced significantly the flow of untreated sewage into the bay. The problem is that those gains have been hard-fought and incremental; meanwhile, the bay has continued to suffer torrential assaults from every imaginable direction.

Here at Bolivar Flats, at the seaward margin of the bay with the renewing ocean tide sluicing past, it was still possible to imagine a coastal wilderness. There were immense numbers of avocets and black-necked stilts feeding in the shallows, and beyond them a raft of white pelicans wavered like a mirage in the hazy, heat-refracted light. The piping plovers—representing 10 percent of the dwindling world population of their species—stood about on one leg with their beaks under their wings, or shuffled the sand with their feet in an attempt to uncover the boreholes of worms.

Eubanks was worried about a proposal to remove sand from Bolivar Flats and transplant it to the chronically eroded Galveston beaches. That was the last thing the plovers needed. Their nesting areas on the eastern seaboard were already seriously threatened by development, and now their critical wintering habitat on the flats was in jeopardy too. It was only one more example, one more way in which some modest industrial or recreational enhancement imperiled the vitality of the bay.

"It's real subtle, it's real incremental," Eubanks said. "We're just picking away at the bay. Every marina, every bulkhead, every little sewage plant, every gallon of effluent—it all has its effect. If you asked me right now, I'd say that in thirty years this bay is going to be a saltwater bathtub."

A bay like Galveston Bay has a limited allegiance to the ocean. Some bays are all salt, simple nicks in the shore-line filled with undiluted seawater. Galveston Bay is more complicated. It depends upon the Gulf of Mexico but at the same time defends itself against it, controlling the intrusions of the open sea through the nearly closed gates of its marine passes.

The bay seeks a certain balance: enough salt water to sustain marine creatures in the first place, enough fresh water to keep them safe from saline-dependent preda-

tors. The big oyster reefs, for instance, tend to be concentrated in the center of the bay, where the saltwater content is characteristically around twenty parts per thousand. That is a congenial enough environment for oysters—which can survive in waters as low as ten parts per thousand—but the salt mixture is too thin to support the various snails and parasites that prey on them.

The ratio of fresh water to salt water is preserved not by delicate adjustments but by erratic and wholesale fluctuation, by floods and storms and by powerful un-seen currents that move beneath the surface. A spring freshet can bring 100,000 cubic feet per second of fresh water into the bay, driving the salt water back into the Gulf. During the drier months of the fall the salt water creeps back, exposing the oyster reefs and brackish marshes to a host of predators that could not normally tolerate such feeble salinity.

By contrast, the routine tides in Galveston Bay are marginal events. In the upper parts of the bay the tide is usually measured in inches, though near the mouth it can be as great as three feet. Compared with the wind, the tide is negligible. The bay's fetch—the vast unobstructed tabletop it presents to the atmosphere—provides a light wind with room to maneuver and grow, allowing it to build waves and send them snowballing across the water's surface. The bay is so susceptible to the effects of wind that a strong winter front can push half—literally half— of its water out into the Gulf.

It is not just the wind that moves the water. The bay is full of mysterious currents that rove silently beneath the surface like some undetectable species of leviathan. These are called density currents—the result of the constant mixing of fresh water and salt water. Because salt water is dense, it sinks to the bottom of the bay and forms a wedge that flows beneath the lighter fresh water, generating a current in the way that a discrepancy in atmospheric pressure generates wind. The greater the depth, the greater the inrush of salt water. The bay's natural depth is anywhere from three to ten feet, but the Houston Ship Channel—which cuts through the bottom of the bay like a giant furrow—is a forty-foot-deep corridor that acts as a saltwater conduit, allowing water from the Gulf to be drawn deep into the bay.

As an estuary, Galveston Bay depends not only on a proper salinity ratio but on the safe harbor its marshes provide for the voyaging planktonic forms that will one day grow into mollusks or fish or anemones. From a distance—as you drive along the Interstate 45 causeway leading to Galveston or across the tidal rivers and bayous farther north—the wetlands that remain along the margins of the bay resemble a lush green mat, as solid and vivid as Astroturf. Up close, they are a mass of solitary spiky plants, thick-bodied stalks of grass that rise from the water like the trees of a flooded forest. The plants are smooth cordgrass, *Spartina alterniflora.* They thrive here, where hardly any other vegetation does. They reproduce by rhizomes that tunnel through the submerged mud. Their cells are dense with salt, giving them the osmotic muscle to suck fresh water from the briny swamp in which they stand.

The cordgrass is hardy but imperiled. Bulkheads, marinas, docks, boat slips, power plants, refineries, parking lots—almost any way in which the bay's resources are customarily tapped leads to the depletion of its primogenitive wetlands. Without the cordgrass, the waves undercut and erode the shoreline, they carry off the land itself—a ranch pasture, the precious square inches fronting a vacation home—and add it into the sediment stew of the bay.

One afternoon I went on a tour of a cordgrass reclamation project near Anahuac, along the eastern shore of the bay, with Bob Nailon, a county extension agent, and Eddie Seidensticker, who works for the Soil Conservation Service. As a team they displayed a touching enthusiasm for the wonders of *Spartina alterniflora,* and kept finishing one another's sentences as we drove in a pickup to the sites where they had been replanting cordgrass. This side of the bay, which consists of a blunt peninsula that finally tapers down to the little fishing and oystering community of Smith Point, seemed light-years away from the heavy industry across the water. We traveled through undeveloped savannahs and spindly forests of Chinese tallow, passing boat slips where Vietnamese fishermen were trailering boats filled with crab pots. The land around here belonged to a few ancestral ranching families, and it had an air of deliberate isolation. Plans to connect Smith Point with Clear Lake City via Hovercraft had been lingering in the air for a few years, but it seemed as if they would linger indefinitely.

"What we're trying to do," Seidensticker said as we drove along a ranch road that paralleled the eroded shoreline, "is reestablish the estuarine zone that used to be here."

That zone was definitely long gone. The shore was an ugly heap of riprap that had not succeeded in keeping the bay from eating the ranch acreage. Up ahead, however, we stopped at a place where the Soil Conservation Service had replanted cordgrass thirty years earlier. The contrast was startling. To our right was a ruined shoreline where the bay water washed through rusted car bodies and tires and buckled sections of concrete that the landowner had deposited over the years in a vain attempt to hold back the wave action. To our left was an appealing expanse of *Spartina* extending thirty or forty yards into the bay, the water smooth except for a little passing shiver caused by a school of fish.

"See," Nailon explained, "the grass acts as a shock absorber. It stops the waves before they impact the bank."

"And when you compare the unsightliness of this," Seidensticker said, indicating the riprap, "to that . . ."

I didn't know whether to be comforted by the comeback of the cordgrass or merely appalled that for so long people had thought so little of the bay that the idea of tossing old car parts into it was perfectly acceptable. Nailon and Seidensticker, however, stood there admiring the cordgrass with the deep contentment of gardeners who had raised a flawless crop of tomatoes. The grass was protected from wave action by a fence made of nylon parachute webbing. When the area was first replanted thirty years ago, no wave barriers had been put up, and Seidensticker and Nailon regarded it as serendipitous that the fledgling cordgrass had survived.

"If you've got a small area of fetch," Seidensticker explained, "if you don't have very much open water, this stuff's easy to grow. But here on Galveston Bay we're talking about a fetch of eight to ten miles. You get a wave three or four feet high, and it just knocks it out."

Originally, they constructed their wave barriers out of used Christmas trees. Seidensticker recalled those days as being "labor-intensive." The parachute webbing was a better solution, cheaper in the long run and more effective. And through trial and error they've learned not to transplant grass in clumps, which disturbs the substrate and makes it more difficult for the grass to take hold. Now the high school and college students who do the planting are instructed to insert each stem individually, setting it lovingly into a six-inch hole poked into the mud.

I borrowed a pair of rubber wading boots from Nailon and walked out into the marsh, noting how firm the sediment was close to shore and how mushy it felt as I walked farther out into the less-established fringes, where the wave energy was stronger and more apt to rile the bottom. Standing at the edge of the marsh, I tracked a series of six-inch-high waves as they moved from the open bay into the *Spartina*. It was a surprisingly beautiful thing to see, the way the unruly waves were tamed bit by bit as they passed through the marsh, growing smaller and more elegant until finally they no longer existed. The waves that hit the outlying stems of cordgrass with such bluster never even touched the shore; they just slouched with their filtered water into a clear backside pool whose firm bottom was crisscrossed with snail tracks and the molted shells of crabs. The thick stalks of the cordgrass were decorated with periwinkle shells, the snails clinging above the waterline and feeding on the algae deposited by the tide. In time the periwinkles would be eaten by redfish and black drum, the fish imbibing the shells and grinding them to powder in a special organ, tough as a drill bit, harbored deep in their throats. And when the cordgrass itself broke down, it would be eaten by micro-organisms that would, in turn, feed the zooplankton and infant fish sheltered in the marsh.

Part of that zooplankton consisted of oyster larvae. At this stage of their lives oysters are known as veligers, simple transparent forms that ingest diatoms as they waft through the submerged cordgrass. There are a lot of them. A single female oyster is capable of producing 500 million eggs in a single year. During spawning season the males are hard at work as well, pumping like underwater geysers and sending out clouds of sperm to mix with the drifting ova. Only a small percentage of the eggs are fertilized, and the resulting veligers have only a dim chance of surviving into oysterhood. After twelve or fourteen days the veligers begin to spat, settling to the bottom of the bay and feeling with their single blob of a foot for a receptive hard surface—known as cultch—on which to settle. Most of the downward-drifting veligers never find a cultch site. They sink into the soft mud like doomed paratroopers. Those that survive land, more often than not, on the shells of other oysters and become part of the reef, cementing themselves for life and de-pending on the currents and tides to bring them food.

In times of floods and heavy rain the oyster population suffers heavy casualties, since prolonged exposure to fresh water saps them of vital minerals. But in the long run fresh water is the oysters' salvation, since it keeps away predatory snails and parasites that could, if uncontrolled, destroy all the oysters in the bay.

"Oysters can be destroyed by a flood, but they'll come back faster than the predators will," says Sammy Ray, a marine biologist with Texas A&M at Galveston. "The last thing you want in an estuary is a stable situation. Show me an area where oysters are not threatened by floods, and I'll show you an area where you don't get consistent oyster production."

Galveston Bay produces two thirds of the oysters harvested in Texas, though as a shellfish industry, oystering runs a distant second to shrimping. Oyster season lasts from November to April, and most of the oyster fishermen are shrimpers during the rest of the year. As a business, oystering is problematic. Oysters are easy prey, but their numbers can fluctuate wildly, and oystermen are constantly under scrutiny from a host of regulatory agencies. The health department has permanently closed more than half of the bay to oyster harvesting and closes other areas when rainfall and runoff threaten to foul the water. (Since oysters are sedentary filter-feeders, they are perfect bacterial sumps—"miniature sewage-treatment plants," one scientist described them—and in even mildly polluted waters they can bank enough germs to greatly enhance a diner's chances of contracting hepatitis.) In November 1987, in a decision that generated much controversy and bitterness, the Texas Parks and Wildlife Department decided that the reefs were in danger of being fished out and closed the oyster season altogether.

"This is a very typical day in terms of politicking," Joe

Nelson told me one day near the end of the oyster season when I visited his operation in Smith Point. "Every day you're fighting for your life."

Nelson's grayish slicked-back hair and flattened nose gave him a dangerous countenance, but he was friendly and related his bureaucratic trials with a touch of exasperated humor. His problems that day had to do with the health department and its decision to close part of the bay after a recent rainfall.

"See," he said, "they took a sample on Tuesday and closed the bay on the assumption that it would be bad. Well, the sample came back Thursday, and it was good, but that was no guarantee that the water wasn't bad on Friday, Saturday, Sunday, and Monday. So then they assume that the water was bad all the way up to Monday and that by now the oysters haven't had time to cleanse themselves. The point is, there was no verification that the water was bad when they closed it, and by the time they find out whether it was or not, it'll be twelve or thirteen days before we're back to work."

As I was straining to understand all of that, Nelson took me on a tour of his dockside facilities, the freezers and shucking tables and piles of fly-infested oyster shell that would be returned to the bay to provide new cultch.

"I've been playing with oysters ever since I was six or seven years old," Nelson reflected, idly sorting through a pile of oyster shell. He said he was born in Galveston in 1936, trundled into a suitcase a few days later, and brought home to Smith Point on a boat.

"Everything was water here," he remembered. "There was very little done by road. We got electricity here in '49. Got phones in '59. Got a shell road in '47 or '48.

"All this shoreline along this bay front where we're

at—you could go out there and pick up all the oysters you wanted to deal with. If the tide was low, the chain of reefs would start at Ellum Grove and go all the way to the Ship Channel. There were so many reefs, there were only three passes through the bay—Barrell Pass, Moody's Cut, and the Ship Channel. Then the shell dredges came in and removed all these shell reefs and barrier islands."

The oysters began to decline as more and more dredging and development altered their habitat. Lake Livingston, built on the Trinity in the sixties, reduced the flow of fresh water at about the same time that a newly dug fish pass on Bolivar Peninsula increased the ratio of salt water. Meanwhile, more and more of the shallow-water reefs were declared off limits by the health department.

These days Nelson's oyster crews spend their time working reefs that Nelson leases from Parks and Wildlife. The work involves not just dredging up oysters but also sometimes shuttling them around, moving them from a section of the bay the health department considers polluted to cleaner water, where they can be purged for two weeks and then harvested for sale.

Joe and his brother, Ben, took me out in a boat to see one of the oyster dredges. The water in the boat slip was a dark green, like a gumbo overloaded with filé powder. As soon as the prop started turning, the mud roiled up to the surface.

"When I was a kid," Joe lamented, "you could see bottom in four, four and a half feet of water. This bay was like a crystal. You could herd redfish, watching everything that was going on. You'd see flounders down there, stingarees. That was before all the sulphur boats destroyed all the grass beds. And you've got bottom down here that's never firmed up from all the dredging."

We pulled out of the channel, the Vingt-et-un Islands on our right and the open bay ahead. The Nelsons' leases were in East Bay, just around the point, their boundaries marked with saplings that rose six feet out of the water and gave the locations a spectral, swampy look.

Over the roar of the engine Joe and Ben hollered complaints into my ear about bureaucratic interference. In fifteen minutes we pulled up to a long barge-like vessel with an overhead awning. The boat was just then hauling up its dredge, which resembled a massive enclosed rake. We went aboard and watched the crew break apart the clusters of oysters on the sorting table. An oyster has to be three inches long before it's legal, and many of the smaller ones were cemented to the shells of the keepers. Mixed in with the clusters were the cone-shaped shells of the predator snails called oyster drills, and many of the oysters themselves were infested with tiny sponges that had bored into their shells and left a signature resembling that of a ringworm.

The Nelsons took along a dozen good-sized oysters when they returned to their boat. While Ben steered, Joe pried one open with a pocketknife.

"See how yellow it is here?" he said, pointing to the swollen protoplasm of the oyster, its heart pumping beneath a glaze of mucus. "He's done started to release his gonads. When he's caught for too long in fresh water he'll feed on his body fluid, use up all his gonadal material to support his life.

"An oyster's always doing one of two things. He's either laying down shell or he's using up shell. See those little brown spots there? That's where a predator's trying to come in and he's laying down shell to prevent it."

Joe stood for a moment studying the oyster. "You know, the more I learn about him and his reproductive cycle, his great ability to withstand predators, his ability to shrink his shell up when conditions aren't right—he's just an amazing creature. I can take this oyster out of the shell and leave him on the half shell and he'll start laying down a crust of a shell on there. As far as I know I'm the only one who's ever experimented with that. I've had 'em stay alive for six weeks on the half shell. He'll be ugly as the devil, but at least he's alive and well."

Joe looked admiringly at the oyster one last time and then slurped him off the shell.

On the way back to Smith Point the Nelsons complained anew about Parks and Wildlife and the way the health department habitually closed the bay at the first hint of rainfall ("Every time a cow pisses on a flat rock," Ben said, "we get alarmed"), but their mood was high as they downed the rest of the oysters.

"This is the only way to live," Joe said, prying apart another shell as Ben opened up the throttle. "Salt water in your face all day, every day of your life."

The main channel of the Trinity River enters the bay through a green delta land braided together with dozens of wandering, nameless streams. Here, miles above the bay itself, are standing lakes bordered by cypress, the water bubbling with methane gas when you disturb the fecund bottom with an oar. Alligators plunge into the water at the approach of a boat, sending an agitated streak of mud outward from the bank.

This is the country—bayous and swamps and verdant lowlands—that feeds the bay. Down these streams, over these grasslands, comes the crucial freshwater inflow, bearing with it the plant detritus that provides the diet of the zooplankton waiting in the *Spartina* marsh. Anything that alters or interrupts this flow threatens, in small or large measure, the fundamental character of Galveston Bay.

No one knows for sure just how great an effect the construction of the Wallisville reservoir might have on the bay, but driving a stake through the heart of this project has been a cherished goal of environmentalists for decades. As originally conceived in the late fifties, Wallisville was a 19,000-acre reservoir that would have inundated almost the entire delta of the Trinity River and provided the first lock for the Trinity River barge canal, a wildly ambitious notion then in vogue whose purpose was to connect Fort Worth to the sea. The U.S. Army Corps of Engineers began construction on the dam and the lock in 1966 and was just about finished in 1973 when a federal judge, agreeing with the Sierra Club and other plaintiffs that the Corps' environmental impact statement had been inadequate, issued an injunction. The Corps went back to the drawing board and returned with a modified proposal, one that would reduce the impounded acreage to one fourth of what it had been in the original plan. The justification for the dam had been changed too. Since the Trinity barge canal had been shelved, the dam was now billed as a means for controlling saltwater intrusions into the water supply of the rice farmers along the lower Trinity. After years of courtroom intrigue, the injunction was finally lifted, but in the meantime the federal government—which under the Reagan administration regarded water-supply issues as a local responsibility—had backed out of its original agreement to foot most of the bill.

For the dam to be finished, somebody needs to pay for it. The City of Houston, whose water supply would benefit from the reservoir, is the likeliest entity to pick up the tab, but for now the project is dormant once again, and there are a lot of people who would like to see it never wake up.

"It's not an environmental disaster," insists Bill Wooley, the chief planner of the Corps of Engineers. "You've got to remember, this dam is only four feet high. It's not a Grand Coulee. Unfortunately the word 'dam' at the mouth of the Trinity sets off an emotional reaction in people that we'll be stopping the flow. But it's like putting a teacup at the end of a hose. Once that teacup is full, the rest of the water runs around."

A retired real estate agent named John Cheesman took me upriver one day in his custom-made johnboat. He was anti-dam and he seldom passed up the opportunity to show a reporter or interested visitor the site of the impending debacle. When we were a few miles upstream from Anahuac, a squall passed over the boat and Cheesman broke out a pair of sou'westers. In the wake of the squall there were terns and white ibis flying over the channel and mullet slipping out of the water with effortless velocity.

"How big the reservoir is or isn't is irrelevant," Cheesman said, as he turned off the main channel. "The point is you're destroying the dynamics of the river, you're changing the nature of the water. Think of all that vegetative matter in the Trinity River bottom. As it dies, the floodwaters of the river come in and flush it out into the bay. Sure, water will still pour out over the top of the dam, but all the plant detritus—the food base for those juvenile crabs and shrimp in the bay—will settle down to the bottom."

He steered the boat into the marsh grass and cut the motor when the bow hit solid ground. Ahead of us, a few paces away, were the remains of the original Wallisville dam. It was a harmless-looking thing, a long ribbon of concrete that appeared to be no higher than a curb. The lake that would result from the dam, if it were ever built, would be no deeper in most places than four feet.

"It's not the kind of thing," Cheesman offered sarcastically, "that looks like a monument to man's ingenuity."

I was struck by how such a modest structure, located miles upriver from the entrance to Galveston Bay, could have such potentially profound effects on that massive body of water. For all the degradation it had endured, the bay had always seemed somehow impervious to me. I had assumed that when it came time for the bay to die, it would die of some titanic environmental insult that would be worthy of its grandeur. But I realized, standing here on the low concrete spillway of the abandoned dam, that the end would probably not be that dramatic. Galveston Bay was like a beating heart whose veins and capillaries were being closed off, almost unnoticeably, one by one. In the end no one would be able to tell exactly when or why the blood stopped flowing.

The bottom of Galveston Bay, if you could remove the water to inspect it, would appear to be crisscrossed with deep gouges. These are the avenues upon which the commerce of the bay travels, the channels through which heavy oceangoing vessels move along like slot cars on a toy roadway. In Audubon's time the bay was navigable only at high tide, and it was a common occurrence for boats to run aground on the bars and oyster reefs. In 1870 a six-foot-deep channel was cut through the shell islands in the middle of the bay, and dredging has been going on ever since. The Houston Ship Channel, which runs from the buoy outside of Bolivar Roads all the way to the turning basin at the far-inland Port of Houston, has been steadily deepened over the years to accommodate ever-larger classes of vessels.

Improving and maintaining navigational waterways is the work of the U.S. Army Corps of Engineers. The Corps loves its work. It exists to implement plans—to build, to dredge, to shore up, to move earth and to divert water. At the behest of the Port of Houston, the Corps is now planning to deepen the Houston Ship Channel by ten feet—to a total depth of fifty feet—and to increase its width to six hundred feet. The port and the Corps maintain that in order to be cost-effective the channel must be accessible to larger vessels. They also contend that the present width of the channel is a potential safety hazard (though collisions and groundings have declined in recent years as a result of a downward trend in overall tonnage).

"It cannot be allowed," says Jim Blackburn, an environmental lawyer and the chairman of the Galveston Bay Foundation, a newly formed alliance of individuals and corporations whose purpose is to monitor the welfare of the bay. "You're talking about sixty-nine million cubic yards of dredge soil in open disposal. They're going to cover eleven thousand acres of Galveston Bay—that's five percent of the bay—with four feet of muck. All of it uncontained, not diked."

The project, according to its opponents, will markedly increase the turbidity of the bay, disrupt the habitats of benthic creatures like worms and clams that form the base of the bay's food chain, and create a conduit that would enhance the saltwater flow from the Gulf. The process of deepening the channel also has the potential of digging up and redistributing toxic pollutants that have settled down peaceably over the decades into the soft sediment.

Waiting for me back at the Corps office in Galveston were the five volumes of the environmental impact statement on the Ship Channel project, hundreds of pages in which the Corps' in-house biologists, chemists, and environmental managers coolly rebutted the grim predictions of lasting harm that the deepening and widening would bring down upon the bay. The Corps' critics—a category that included much of the membership of the Galveston Bay Foundation—regarded those conclusions with skepticism if not outright hostility. It was painfully obvious that the Corps did not meet its payroll by not building things. "The U.S. Army Corps of Engineers," reads a snide bumper sticker, "Ruining Tomorrow Today."

"Okay, we're not the Sierra Club," Ed White, a public affairs officer with the Corps, told me as we motored up the Ship Channel in an air-conditioned launch. "We're a pragmatic organization, and we're in the position where it's real easy to make us out to be a villain. But our people live here, they work here. This," he said, indicating the vast gray fabric of the bay ahead, "is our recreation area as well as everyone else's."

The boat emerged from the protection of the pass into the open bay, cruising above an invisible crossroads where the Houston Ship Channel, the Galveston Ship Channel, the Texas City Ship Channel, and the Gulf Intracoastal Waterway all converged at the bottom of the bay.

"It gets real busy around here," Floyd Kuykendall, the captain of the launch, said. "You got three or four ferries coming in sometimes. Ships coming in, ships going out."

Shrimp boats lined the channel, and we passed shell barges and drilling rigs and gas wells. A tanker, the *Mobil Vanguard,* slowly bore down upon us from the opposite direction.

"If we were a ship that size," White said, "we'd be heading straight for its nose, and at the last minute we'd veer off and depend on that bow wake to keep us apart. That's because the channel's so narrow. You can imagine what would happen if one of us miscalculated. That's one of the main reasons we have for wanting to widen the channel."

The west shore of the bay, as we cruised by Texas City, was studded with anti-scenery—Monsanto, Arco, Union Carbide. Farther up, the landscape softened somewhat, and as we approached Kemah and Seabrook we could see expensive sailboats pouring from the mouth of Clear Lake. At Atkinson Island, across from Morgan's Point, Kuykendall pulled up at the dock, and White and I got off to look around. The island was a low shell bank that over the years had been enlarged considerably by the dumping of dredge material (the Corps does not like to use the word "spoil"). A circulation channel had been cut through the center of the island, and a gas pump station with its unlit burn-off stack stood at the southern end like a lighthouse. White and I stood on a fetid little beach, looking out over the circulation channel, the noise of the pumping station in the background. The dredge material beneath our feet felt as mucky as quicksand, and the paltry tide of the bay had chipped out a little bluff crowned with sea wrack and trash. White pointed to a congregation of plovers just around the point.

"Those birds have found something to feed on," he said. "This is a real good environment for wildlife."

He had a point, since some spoil islands in the bay have become critical habitats for beleaguered shorebirds, but I was saddened by a deeper implication. I thought of Audubon—"Ah, my dear friend, would that you were here just now to see the Snipes innumerable, the Blackbirds, the Gallinules, and the Curlews that surround us . . ."—and realized that one measure of how relentlessly we had abused Galveston Bay was our benumbed willingness to regard this bogus, pitiful little island as a blessing.

Standing there, I was not particularly filled with hope. It seemed to me that the ruin of Galveston Bay had, from the beginning, been a done deal. It was not clear whether Wallisville and the Ship Channel projects would ever be completed or what effects they would have on the bay if they were. But they embodied an attitude toward the Texas environment that was a long way from dying out, an attitude that at its root accepted the welfare of the bay as a secondary consideration and not as an essential premise. Perhaps the design of these and other projects could be fine-tuned enough that the damage was negligible, but in the end that was not the point. We needed to do something besides ameliorate harm; we needed to restore the bay, to reach some sort of psychic point where we could no longer allow ourselves to believe that there could be, for example, four acceptable categories of polluted water. Finally, the greatest threat to Galveston Bay was our historic inability to regard it not just as a material resource but as a spiritual one.

Time and again I drove the perimeter of the bay, from the isolated mud flats of San Luis Pass to the dense industrial canals leading to the Port of Houston. I liked the bay best in the morning, when the water was so still that boats seemed to glide across its surface like sleds on ice. I rode back and forth on the Bolivar Ferry, watching pods of dolphins as they traveled into the bay from the open Gulf. Once I visited the rookery islands in West Bay, where the salt cedars were stratified with nesting birds—great blue herons on top, white ibis, roseate spoonbills, and common egrets below. At the shoreline royal terns were gathered together in the family grouping that biologists label a creche. A fledgling reddish egret, too young to take precautions, grazed my ear with the tip of its wing; it looked like a cartoon bird, with its wobbly flight and the baby plumage growing in haywire tufts from its head.

In some essential way, however, the bay continued to elude me. There was no prominence from which to view it, and most of the municipalities that depended for their economic health on its proximity seemed to look away from it, oriented instead toward the inland complex of highways and office buildings that the bay's bounty had helped create. It was, I began to realize, a backyard bay whose grandeur was hard to glimpse.

Wanting a more intimate acquaintance, I decided to go fishing for speckled trout in Trinity Bay, several miles downstream from the mouth of the river. My guide was Gene Campbell, a forty-year-old native of Baytown who had been fishing these waters since he was a kid.

The water in this part of the bay was fairly clear—two and a half feet of visibility—and the shoreline was dominated by great homes set back on green manicured bluffs. After running north for ten minutes, Campbell cut the motor and let the boat drift idly in the outgoing tide. Below us, out of sight, an oyster reef ran perpendicular to the shore.

"Trout are visual feeders ninety percent of the time," he said, running a hook through the tail of a live shrimp. "They're on sight attack. They don't feed well unless they can see. That's why we look for water with some visibility to it."

We could see cabbageheads a foot or so under the water, drifting seaward in the tide. Mullet were popping up everywhere. One of them headed straight for the boat, bounding in and out of the water like a skipping stone, and when the fish saw the boat, it changed course in midair. Campbell got a strike right away but lost the trout. When he reeled in his hook the shrimp was still on, folded into a U shape, its rows of feet barely waggling.

Campbell speculated that a young trout had probably attacked the bait from behind, folding it over to avoid the sharp horn projecting from the shrimp's head. Older fish wouldn't have been so delicate. A full-grown trout tends to wolf down fish, including other trout, up to a foot long.

They are serious predators, which I didn't fully appreciate until I boated one a few moments later and looked down its bony yellow gullet. Two long, pointed teeth—made for gripping rather than slashing prey—hung down from its upper jaw. The fish made a desperate croaking noise, expelling air from its bladder, and continued to croak after Campbell tossed it into an ice chest.

We caught five or six more fish, all of them trout. The fish were biting, but they were picky.

"The tide's slowing down now," Campbell said. "They're getting less active and more selective."

He decided to move off the reef and head for the open, hoping to encounter a slick or a "mudball," which would indicate a school of fish feeding with more abandon. The sky was overcast, however, and growing darker, and without the sunshine to highlight a slick, it was difficult to read what was going on beneath the surface.

"We'll go up on that well," Campbell decided. "See if we can't pick up a few fish before we get shoved out of the bay by this storm." He anchored about twenty yards away from a small offshore rig, and we cast toward the wellhead. The bottom there, he explained, would be reinforced with shell, creating a small patch reef attractive to fish. Campbell reeled in a good-sized trout, but after that we had no luck.

"A lot of times at these wellheads," he explained, "we'll catch one fish, and that's it. It may be because there's just one fish there. The question I have is, What's he doing there by himself? Is he a sentry? A bait scout? They're school fish. They have no business being by themselves."

At this time of the year the trout were through spawning in the warm water along the shore. Unlike redfish, which move out into the turbulence of the Gulf surf to spawn, trout are lifelong denizens of the bay. Born in the marshy fringes, they school up and move out into open water after eight or ten months, following the salinity gradients and moving into deeper or shallower water as the temperature suits them. They prey on shad or other fish, and during the fall, when the year's hatch of white shrimp scuttles forth out of the marshes, the trout are there waiting for them, causing the frightened shrimp to leap out of the water like grasshoppers.

"The little fish are the easiest to catch," Campbell said. "They eat more often, their metabolism's faster. A ten-pound trout'll eat a two-pound mullet and digest it for a week. A little one-and-a-half- to two-pound trout, though, he'll eat eight shrimp a day. That's eight feedings, eight chances he'll take your hook."

The sky grew darker as we fished the wellhead, and we could see lightning striking the ground near Smith Point. We reeled in our lines and ran ahead of the storm, stopping near an oil separator to try once more before going in. But the storm was coming on fast, and the sound of the separator's compressor was lost to the increasing rumble of thunder. The air was charged and calm. Static electricity caused our fishing lines to bow upward from the surface of the water.

"Notice how we've got the bay to ourselves?" Campbell said. I looked and saw that there were no other boats on the water. The storm clouds were rapidly engulfing the shoreline and contracting the horizon, so that the refineries and offshore rigs were no longer visible. All that we could see was the gray, marly surface of the bay, beginning to rile as the wind came up out of the stillness. The bay seemed in command of all this atmospheric power—it seemed ageless and, though I knew better, inviolable. I reeled in my line slowly, not wanting to go, and listened as the last dying trout flapped about desperately in the ice chest.

Taking Care of
Lonesome Dove

There sat the town of Lonesome Dove: a dozen grim buildings made of adobe and faded lumber, a single desolate street teeming with dust devils and undercut with dry washes, a vulture coasting above the twilit Rio Grande. The town was perched on a high cutbank above the river, affording it a panoramic view of the mesquite flats on the Mexican side. In the evening stillness I could hear cattle lowing and red-winged blackbirds rustling in the canebrakes, and the percussive sound of a bass launching itself out of the water.

A group of horsemen came riding from one end of the street toward the deep wash that led down to the river. They were seated on antique high-backed saddles and armed with horse pistols and Henry repeating rifles and Green River skinning knives. The horses looked as lanky and weathered as the men who rode them, and the spectacle of them wading into the tranquil river in the charged evening light was so exhilarating that for a moment it was possible to disregard the crowd of camera operators, grips, sound men, lighting technicians, script supervisors, and wranglers that testified to the somewhat dispiriting fact that it was all just a movie.

The riders were halfway across the river when the director yelled, "Cut!" Escorted by a half-dozen watchful wranglers, the actors turned their horses around to the American side and led them back up the bank to the starting position for another take. The pounding of hooves against the soft earth produced a deep, satisfying rumble, and though the actors chatted and joked among themselves as they spurred their horses up the street the illusion of authenticity would not go away—any reader of Larry McMurtry's vast novel could have stood in this dusty make-believe town southeast of Del Rio and checked off the cast of characters as they rode past.

There was Woodrow F. Call, the emotionally withheld former Texas Ranger whose iron will sets into motion the star-crossed trail drive that is the heart of the story. As Call, Tommy Lee Jones wore a black round-top hat and a white beard that put me in mind—not inappropriately—of Captain Ahab. Behind him rode Robert Duvall as the loquacious and magnificent Augustus McCrae. Then came Robert Urich as Jake Spoon, Danny Glover as Joshua Deets, D. B. Sweeney as Dish Boggett, Tim Scott as Pea Eye, Ricky Schroder as Newt . . . all of them splendidly grungy in their chaps caked with fuller's earth (to provide the illusion of even more trail dust than

they had actually accumulated), in their faded bandannas and their sweat-stained hats with artfully frayed and
moth-eaten brims.

"Don't they look great?" Bill Wittliff, *Lonesome
Dove*'s screenwriter and executive producer, asked as we
stood there eating dust. "Don't they look just wonderful?" The mood on the set was high at this hour, with the
day's work almost done and the light growing more
gorgeous by the minute.

"Getting some good stuff, Bill!" Robert Duvall declared to Wittliff as he moseyed over after the final take.
Duvall was startlingly Gus. I had seen him a few nights
earlier in *Colors*, and the memory of him as a middle-
aged Los Angeles police officer was still strong enough
for me to marvel at the swiftness of the transition. It
seemed that in a matter of only days he had realigned his
body, changed from a bulky cop with a low center of
gravity to a rangy, hollow-cheeked cowman with decidedly bowed legs. He was full of an actor's enthusiasms
tonight, praising the cinematographer, discussing the
pacing of an upcoming scene, describing a passage in a
book he'd read about how a group of Texas Rangers,
ambushed during a river crossing, broke down and cried
like babies at the death of their leader.

Duvall had a wonderful role to play. In the course of
this movie Gus McCrae would rescue Lorena Wood
(Diane Lane) from the appallingly villainous Blue Duck
(Frederic Forrest), slam a surly bartender's head onto the
bar of a saloon, engage in two desperate Indian battles,
and die a heartbreaking and unforgettable death in Miles
City, Montana. These events seemed written already into
Duvall's face, into his whole aspect; you could see the
claim the character of Gus had not only on the actor's

attention but in some magical way upon his being. Tonight, however, he was ebullient. Standing there bow-legged, his thumbs hooked in his gunbelt, Duvall lifted himself off the ground in an irrepressible hop.

It was an article of faith on the set of *Lonesome Dove* that this would not be an ordinary movie. Logistics alone moved it out of that category: an eight-hour television miniseries with a budget of almost $20 million, a big-name cast, and a devastating sixteen-week shooting schedule involving dozens of sets, massive location shifts, eighty-nine speaking parts, and up to 1,400 head of stampeding cattle. Though it was destined for the small screen, the film's scale was vast, a throwback to those bygone days when cinematic behemoths like *Giant* and *The Alamo* still grazed in the pastures of Texas myth.

But *Lonesome Dove* was special not just for its scale but for its source material. Larry McMurtry's Pulitzer Prize–winning novel is an epic compendium of Texas history, folklore, and cherished bits of cultural identity. Though the novel borrows elegantly from a variety of sources—trail drive memoirs, the works of J. Frank Dobie, the historical friendship of Charles Goodnight and Oliver Loving, even old movies—its own singular vision is never in question. Overlong, slow-to-start, *Lonesome Dove* is nonetheless an irresistible book, a ragged classic fueled by McMurtry's passionate regard for his outsized characters and by his poignant reckoning of their limitations. In the space of a few years, it has become the sacred text of Texas literature, and the filmmakers were aware that there were a lot of readers who did not want to see it screwed up.

The role of guardian angel was being played by Bill

Wittliff. I had known Bill for years, long enough to appreciate the fit he and *Lonesome Dove* made. In movie jargon, Wittliff was a hyphenate, a writer-producer-director whose credits over the years have included *The Black Stallion, Barbarosa,* and *Red Headed Stranger.* Most of his films reflected, in one way or another, a preoccupation with the myths and lingering values of the Texas frontier. Like his friend Larry McMurtry, he grew up in rural Texas in the forties and fifties, when it was still possible to witness firsthand the fading pageantry of the open range. (Wittliff remembers standing at his stepfather's graveside after the rest of the mourners had left, watching a relative open the coffin and reverently slip a pair of boots onto the deceased's feet.)

"I think I was the perfect screenwriter for this," he said, digging into the pocket of his jeans for the key to his pickup. "I really do. The people in the book are all Larry's people, but I knew them too. I never got jammed even for a second wondering who these people were or what was at their core. That's one of the things that *Lonesome Dove* is about: the fact that we all somehow believe that those are the guys we came from.

"You've read the screenplay," he said to me in a concerned voice. "Do you think it's faithful to Larry's book?"

It struck me that I'd never heard a screenwriter express that particular concern before. But Wittliff was obviously more than *Lonesome Dove*'s screenwriter or its executive producer. He was its custodian. I had stayed up for three nights with his script and found that in its 373 pages it managed to accommodate all the book's vital particulars while discreetly pruning its shaggy story line. Even the changes had a certain scholarly flourish.

When Wittliff felt he needed a line of dialogue for Call at the end of the movie, for instance, he lifted a quote from Charles Goodnight, the legendary cattleman on whom Call is partly based.

"The thing I keep preaching to everybody," he said, "is that *Lonesome Dove is* the star. If we take care of *Lonesome Dove,* it'll take care of us."

Taking care of *Lonesome Dove* was not a simple proposition. The stampedes and dust storms, the Indian battles and rapes and hangings and river crossings and seething nests of water moccasins—all that would have been difficult enough to film without the logistics behind it: the wardrobe trucks, prop trucks, catering trucks, and motor homes that had to be moved at every change in location; the highboys, Crank-O-Vators, scrims, dinos, baby stands, and ballasts that had to be set up for each shot; the unforeseen details that had to be tended to (biscuits that were not brown enough to match those in the preceding shot, pipes that would not stay lit, moustaches that would not stay on); and then finally the myriad ways in which horses and cattle could be counted on to display their indifference to a film adaptation of an 843-page trail drive novel.

The director of *Lonesome Dove* was Simon Wincer, a forty-four-year-old Australian with a calm demeanor and a kindly, inquisitive expression. He had risen to prominence recently with a pair of films, *Pharr Lapp* and *The Light Horsemen,* that demonstrated a stylish way with narrative and—equally important—a talent for moving large groups of animals around.

"I'm used to large-scale projects," he said as he flipped through a green binder with the day's storyboard and shooting script. "And this one is as epic as they come.

When I came to Texas I realized it was like remaking the Bible."

Though *Lonesome Dove* was a television production, Wincer and Douglas Milsome, his cinematographer, were shooting it like a feature, with sophisticated lighting, moving cameras, and complex staging that required scenes to be shot from up to a half-dozen different angles. The film's fluent intercutting—which would be so thoughtlessly accepted by a viewer's retina—required such laborious repositioning of cameras, lights, and hundreds of accessories that watching it was like watching an army strike camp only to set it up again a few yards away.

One afternoon while the crew was prepping a shot, I went over to talk to Tommy Lee Jones, who was sitting at the base of a six-kilowatt light in the dirt yard of the Hat Creek bunkhouse, idly whacking the ground with a quirt. D. B. Sweeney, who plays the lovesick Dish Boggett, had told me to ask Jones for a recitation of the vinegarroon toast, which Sweeney had termed "a beautiful Texas haiku."

"Hell, yes, I can recite the vinegarroon toast," Jones said. He held up an imaginary shot glass, narrowed his eyes, and declaimed:

"'Here's to the vinegarroon / that jumped on the centipede's back. / He looked at him with a glow and a glee / and he said, "You poisonous son-of-a-bitch, / if I don't git you, you'll git me."'

"You can find that in one of Mr. Dobie's books," Jones explained. "*Cow People,* I believe it is."

At forty-one, Jones was at least a dozen years shy of Woodrow Call's unspecified middle age, but in the midday light he looked pretty close. In addition to the white beard, his face was covered with three layers of latex stipple to simulate wrinkles, and above that were artful depictions of burst capillaries and liver spots.

He described the application of this makeup in authoritative detail, and during the days I spent on the set his conversation touched with equal enthusiasm upon the nature of the bicameral mind, the poetry of William Carlos Williams, the lost Jim Bowie silver mine, the proper technique for flanking a steer, and the art of acting.

"The acting's easy," he said. "It's like anything else—like makin' a pan of biscuits—it's all in the preparation. You have to go through life and find those things that accrue to the big bouillabaisse of your brain. Or the little bouillabaisse, as the case may be."

A Harvard-educated resident of San Saba, Jones projected an appealing air of real-world savvy. His interpretation of Call—a man so interior and taciturn that he cannot even bring himself to acknowledge his own son—seemed to be a shade or two less grim than McMurtry's but authentic all the same. Jones said he had based the character partly on his own two grandfathers, and of course he had read Mr. Haley's book about Mr. Goodnight.

Jones had a booming voice that made me think of Shanghai Pierce, the South Texas cattle baron who bragged that his own voice was "too big for indoor use." The makeup and fringe of white beard did their job in making him look older, but they also lent his ornery features an unexpected mildness. On a horse, he was spectacularly convincing. There was about him a certain unstated pride—a reveling—in the fact that he was a Texan, that the character he was playing came to him not just through research but as a kind of legacy, through his own bones.

"In this next scene," he explained as he was called over for rehearsal, "I come ridin' the Hell Bitch in from over there to where Gus is sittin' on the porch. There's five Hell Bitches in this movie—one to buck, one to bite, one to kick, one to drag around, and one just to stand there."

The Hell Bitch, in the book, is Call's prized but unbroken gray mare. This particular scene called for the horse to come charging wildly into the frame with its rider barely in control—one of many occasions in the filming of the movie in which Jones would be called upon to display his horsemanship.

The braking horse was consistently engulfed in a cloud of dust, though a few million more particles of grit were barely noticeable in the endless sandstorm that plagued the production. The crew, whose faces were often obscured by bandannas and surgical masks, had taken to calling the movie "Lonesome Dust." Every few takes a water truck would drive by to wet down the swirling earth in front of the house, and an assistant camera operator would spray a product called Dust Buster over the moving parts of the Arriflex lens. One of the wardrobe assistants had discovered a pair of orphaned baby jackrabbits, and when the wind was down she would bring them out of the protective pocket of her camp stool and feed them drops of milk from the end of her finger.

Duvall, as Gus, sat on the porch in his weather-beaten hat and faded red undershirt. He seemed oblivious not only to the dust but to all the people and instruments that were crowded inches away from his face. Unlike Jones—

whose attitude toward acting appeared as genial and uncomplicated as that of a high school quarterback who, to be a good sport, had agreed to take the lead in the senior play—Duvall was always taut with concentration. Sitting on the porch between takes, unapproachable and solitary, he muttered his lines under his breath, jerking his head this way or that with the ratchety, quizzical movements of a songbird.

Duvall seemed always to be engaged in some mysterious private rehearsal, some secret summoning act that he employed for even the most cursory scenes. One night I watched as he prepared for a shot that would be merely a cutaway view of Gus walking up to the Dry Bean saloon. Waiting for his cue, bathed in the illumination of a quartz light, Duvall paced back and forth, refining Gus's crotchety stride. Just before "Action" was called he stopped, slapped his thighs, rubbed his hands together, planted his feet, and crouched forward, as tense as a long distance runner at the start of a race.

Occasionally, though, when a scene satisfied him, Duvall would release his grip. "I nailed that scene!" he said after one such take, waltzing past the lights and firing an imaginary six-shooter at the ground. "Pow! Pow! Pow! I nailed it!" At such moments the grizzled and bowlegged Texas Ranger seemed to have fled from Duvall's body like an exorcised spirit, giving it back momentarily to its primary occupant, whoever exactly that was.

The action of *Lonesome Dove* takes place from Texas to Montana, a range of locations that would be prohibitively expensive for any picture, much less one that involves so much livestock and period baggage. Though New Mexico would stand in for many of the more northern locations, one of the things Wittliff insisted upon was that the Texas parts be shot in Texas.

The ranch outside Del Rio on which the production company had set up shop contained 56,000 acres. Within its fence lines were landscapes that could credibly represent anything from desert to brushland to Hill Country glade. Today an impounded stretch of Pinto Creek just upstream from the ranch headquarters was being used as the Canadian River.

The scene to be filmed was described in the screenplay as follows:

EXT. CANADIAN RIVER-MORNING
The Hat Creek cowboys (naked or wearing
only long johns, though all are wearing their hats)
whoop and yell as they swim the herd across the
Canadian River.

It was innocuous-sounding words like those—"swim the herd across the Canadian River"—that presented *Lonesome Dove* with its endless trials in livestock deployment. Down by the creek the Shotmaker—a half-million-dollar four-wheel-drive vehicle with a soaring camera crane—was already in position and workers were shuttling back and forth across the creek in a makeshift ferry in order to set up another camera on the opposite bank.

At the base camp, a quarter mile up the road, some of the actors who were playing the Hat Creek drovers— including Larry McMurtry's son James—stood around in their chaps outside the wardrobe truck, being dusted down with fuller's earth.

In a nearby field Tommy Lee Jones was running the Hell Bitch in figure eights to get her (or him—this particular Hell Bitch was a gelding) into a calm frame of mind.

"Thar's them bovines now," he said, reining up and watching as three hundred head of cattle headed in his direction. The animals' hooves, trotting over the dried brush covering the field, produced a whispery rattling sound that made it seem that the cattle were not bearing down upon the earth with their full weight.

In a perfect world, these would have been Longhorns. But as Jimmy Medearis, the head wrangler, explained to me, Longhorn cattle—particularly cows with calves—are not "maneuverable." For the sake of historical accuracy, Mexican *corrientes* were the next best thing. They were framey, wild-looking beasts with substantial horns, and there were a few in the herd that were as shaggy and humpbacked as buffalo.

The wranglers herded the cattle down to the creek and then escorted them—via a much shallower crossing just upstream—to the top of the high bluff on the far side. Jones, Danny Glover, Ricky Schroder, and the rest of the actors playing the Hat Creek Outfit soon followed.

Jimmy Medearis remained on the near bank, a bag of range cubes hanging across his saddlehorn. He planned to strew the feed into the path of the oncoming cattle to slow them down after the excitement of the crossing. Nearby, an EMT team moved into position.

"This is going to be a hand-on-switch situation," Robert Rooy, the first assistant director, announced. "All three cameras need to be ready. Everybody please clear. Speak up now if you're not ready or forever hold your peace. Stay off the radios, please. No idle chitchat."

There was no apparent motion for a few seconds after Wincer called "Action," but soon a cloud of dust was visible behind the bluff on the other side of the creek.

"Cattle at sixty yards," Rooy said, holding a walkie-talkie to his ear. "Cattle at forty yards. Cattle at twenty yards."

Jones appeared over the bluff first. He was wearing his long underwear and riding the Hell Bitch down the steep embankment with the herd of cattle behind him. The other actors—some of them totally naked except for their hats, others in their long johns—followed, swinging ropes and heyahhing the cattle along to the water.

The herd plunged without complaint into the water and held their stricken faces high while they groped for the bottom with their hooves. Beside them the cowboys struggled to hold on while their horses stroked awkwardly across the narrow creek. In an instant, the pretty green water had changed into a stew of suspended mud and dislodged vegetation.

The crew was applauding as the drovers, sopping wet and buzzing with adrenaline, emerged from the creek.

"That look like a cattle crossin'?" Jones asked Wittliff.

"Damn right it did."

Duvall had not been involved in the river crossing, because in the movie he is waiting for the cowboys on the far bank, having just come back from the various thundering adventures involved in his rescue of Lorena from Blue Duck. In the scene remaining to be shot, he would talk to Call and the others while the cattle crossed the river in the background.

Duvall, Jones, Tim Scott, Ricky Schroder, and D. B. Sweeney retired to their director's chairs in the scattered shade of a huisache and rehearsed the scene in relative peace while the wranglers began recycling the cattle back to the other side of the creek.

"I was sorry to hear about Bill Spettle," Duval said in a recitative, as yet uncommitted voice.

"Same bolt a lightnin' that kilt him kilt thirteen head a cattle," Jones responded, hanging his wet socks up on a limb to dry. "Burned 'em black."

They went through it several more times, waiting for the complicated shot to be set up. When it was ready, Jones and the rest of the drovers who would be emerging from the river rode their horses into the water to get wet again. Duvall sat waiting for them on his horse, enduring numberless pesty adjustments: a makeup man standing on a ladder and combing the hair beneath the actor's hat brim, a camera assistant taking a light reading off his face, a woman from the wardrobe department snapping a Polaroid while another daubed sweat on his back, a boom operator dangling a fur-covered microphone above his head, and a wrangler crouching beneath his horse, holding its tail. Through it all Duvall was as mute and still as an equestrian statue.

All this artifice fell away when the cameras started to roll and Jones and the others rode up from the creek as if they had just crossed with the cattle. The cattle themselves were crossing again for real, and so the background was full of marvelous chaos as Jones and Duvall delivered their lines. The takes were all good, but on the third take something extraordinary happened, something you could not explain. It had to do simply with the way Duvall said the line "I'm sorry we lost Bill Spettle"— the way his voice now seemed to have landed in some new register of compassion and tragic authority.

At that moment I was convinced. Gus and Call seemed utterly real to me, and I was struck with a vague sense of premonition that at first I could not account for. Then I remembered something I had seen the day before, when I had been poking around the set of *Lonesome Dove*. I was in Pumphrey's General Store, admiring the shelves that were stocked with realistic-looking bottles of chill tonic and Chief Two Moons Bitter Oil Laxative, when I wandered into a side room filled with props. Leaning against the wall was a human form, wrapped in burlap and lashed to a board. When I saw that the form had only one booted leg, I realized what it was. It was Gus, who dies of gangrene in Montana and is hauled back by Call to be buried in Texas.

That burlap-wrapped mannequin was an unaccountably poignant sight, as if Gus were real and the body was really Gus. You get confused on a movie set, because for all the chaos and tedium the urge to believe that it is all not just a movie is as strong as it is in a theater. Watching Duvall and Jones speak to each other as Gus and Call now above the noise of the cattle and the whistles and grunts of the drovers, I found myself particularly susceptible. I was sad that Gus would die, sad that Call would end up haunted and bereft, but most of all I was sad because I could not help knowing that the myth they represented, for all its immediacy and ageless power, was still a myth.

When the scene between Gus and Call was finished and the cattle had crossed the river for the seventh and last time, somebody noticed a solitary cow still standing on the other side of the creek.

"I'll get him!" yelled one of the actors, a young bit player still clad only in his cowboy hat and chaps. Swinging his rope, he kicked his horse toward the water.

"Stop!" Jimmy Medearis, the head wrangler, shouted after him. "Let us get him! You guys are *not* cowboys!"

The actor obeyed, but he cast a resentful eye at Medearis. What was the harm in pretending?

Feeling Flush

We find ourselves in Monte Carlo. From the gaudy turrets of the Casino a swarm of bats spirals up into the evening sky over the gardens and seascape terraces that are filled with elderly women walking arm in arm. It is midwinter, sixty degrees Fahrenheit, just cool enough for their leopard coats, real or *faux*. The sovereign principality of Monaco—smaller than New York's Central Park—is so minute, so tidy, that it can be taken in with one quick sweep of the eyes. There is the ancient fortress Rock, with the white flag flying above the palace to indicate that the widowed Prince Rainier III, His Serene Highness, is home. The harbor from which Julius Caesar once sailed is filled now with ponderous yachts, and behind it, creeping upward toward a crowning massif, are shopping streets laid out in irregular tiers and switchbacks.

This evening the Mediterranean and the sky above it share the same deepening hue, so there is no perceptible horizon when we look seaward from the Casino's terrace; just a seamless, hazy void. This vast sheet of water is as calm as an ornamental pond, though now and then a seaborne breeze will touch its surface and cause it to lift and fall in faint, suspirating motions.

Soon, on January 27, it will be the feast day of Saint Dévote, celebrating the arrival on these shores, sixteen centuries ago, of the patron saint of Monaco. According to legend, Dévote was a Christian girl from Corsica who had been tortured and killed by the island's Roman governor. Her friends placed her body in a fishing boat and set it adrift, praying for the winds to deliver her to a Christian country for burial. A storm came up, and the little boat would have been lost had not a dove emerged from the dead girl's mouth and guided the craft to this craggy shoreline at the opening of a steep gorge.

Dévote had the posthumous good fortune to end her journey among the faithful. The Monégasques, as the ancestral population of Monaco is known, buried the girl and built a chapel to her memory, and she in turn responded to their kindness with answered prayers and miraculous cures.

But Monte Carlo is no Lourdes. It is, of course, a prime disporting ground for the world's leisured classes and has been ever since Rainier's ancestor Prince Charles III established the Société des Bains de Mer (Society of Sea Bathing) in 1863. Though Charles was certainly interested in promoting Monte Carlo's already fashionable beaches, the SBM had about as much to do with sea bathing as poor Saint Dévote had to do with recreational boating. This was the Victorian age, however, and it would not have been discreet for Prince Charles to announce his real goal of turning Monaco into the gambling capital of Europe.

The casino he built is an amiable Belle Époque monstrosity whose facade is crowded with sculptural flourishes, from winged men to cupids to trident-wielding water nymphs bursting out of their niches. Opposite is the equally ornate Hôtel de Paris; like the Casino it is strangely, sparklingly clean, so free of grime and so unweathered that it looks more like a theme-park replica than the real thing.

The evening's plans call for a cautious bit of gambling. After the sun has set, after we have eaten a bowl of *soupe de poisson* and injured our gums on the sharp crusts of French rolls, we stroll into the Casino, affecting a Continental nonchalance. Inside it is like a wonderfully overripe art museum—a procession of gilded *salles* with murals depicting scenes of pastoral concupiscence. Across the walls and ceilings romp various maidens, shepherdesses, and sprites, either breezily naked or outfitted in swirling, diaphanous garments. Some of them are picking fruit; some are reclining on clouds; some are languorously smoking cigars.

At this time of year the Casino is thinly populated, a fact that only enhances its native aura of exclusivity. But the place feels surprisingly welcoming. Once a visitor has displayed his passport and paid his admission, he is granted the illusion of being a member of the club. Most of the patrons are feeding francs into the slot machines that are clustered in a side room, but the vulgar sounds of these *machines à sous* are swallowed up in the elegant silence of the main gaming hall. Here the only noise is the whisper of the ivory roulette ball traveling in its wheel of polished wood. Only one table is in operation, and the players crowd around it without excitement, as if it were merely a fire that they had been drawn to for warmth. They are, for the most part, a languid and sleepy-looking assemblage of junior aristocrats—young men with mussed or flowing hair, wearing designer sports jackets that are as shapeless as raincoats. They place their bets, casually sip their drinks while the wheel is spinning, and display the same indifference whether the croupier rewards them or sweeps their chips away with a little rake.

I have allotted myself a grubstake of $20, but I decide it would be an insult to these gentlemen to subject them to the spectacle of my miserly and craven betting, so I merely hover for a while, squinting down at the action as if with a coolly appraising eye, and then it's off to the Loews hotel, in whose rowdier, American-style casino I am able to lose my $20 in an instant without undue embarrassment. There is more action in the Loews casino and no fussy decorum to suppress it. The place is full of middle-class American women sitting on stools and patiently working the slot machines, with onlookers crowding around the jittery shooters at the crap tables. Next door, in La Folie Russe, dancers with whiskers painted on their cheeks are presenting a topless musical number borrowed from *Cats*.

In the morning the sun rises through a sea mist, gradually disclosing the curve of the shore, the hills crowned with self-contained medieval villages and laced with balcony roads, built by Caesar and Napoleon, that lead off into the Italian Alps. No fishing boats bob on the water; no signs of industry or commerce intrude; no sounds are heard except the squawk of Mediterranean gulls. Here, in the pleasure capital of Europe, there is an eerie lack of urgency and motive. One rises in the morning and feels only the call to leisure.

If we were to be serious about getting into the mood of Monte Carlo, we would pass our days in a listless, becalmed state, waiting to dress, waiting to eat, waiting for the Casino to open again so that we could redeem ourselves from last night's stingy betting. But at heart we are bustling American tourists, and so we rouse ourselves and head off to the palace to witness the changing of the guard. To travel on foot from one end of Monaco to the other requires, at a brisk walk, hardly more than an hour, though it's easy to lose your way in the twisted streets or surrender to the impulse to follow some steep, wandering stairway to its hidden terminus. Along the Avenue Princesse Grace, along the Avenue Président J. F. Kennedy, along the Boulevard Albert Premier and the Rue Grimaldi we make our way to the foot of the Rock, the great natural bulwark, whose summit is crowned by a tasteful, rambling palace that looks more like an immense bungalow than a princely castle.

We climb up the steep Rampe Major, the modern city falling away behind us until it is just a cluttered expanse of red-tiled roofs and cream-colored condominium towers. The Mediterranean is hammered flat by the winter sun, and the martial music and pealing bells that accompany the changing of the guard echo across its taut surface all the way to Italy. The ceremony itself is perfunctory, or perhaps just seems so in the heart of the off-season, with so few tourists to witness it. The palace guards wear white spats and blue velvety helmets. Like figures in a cuckoo clock, they emerge from their hiding places to play their instruments, slap their rifles, and bark their commands; and then suddenly they are gone.

The palace shares the promontory of the Rock with Monaco Ville, the principality's oldest residential area. This is a neighborhood of narrow, sunless streets and cavernous shops selling T-shirts and toy roulette games. One of these streets is home to a wax museum depicting the history of Monaco. The museum is a game effort, but the history of Monaco does not lend itself to vivid tableaux. In scene after scene we follow the waxen princes and lords of Monaco as they shake hands with heads of state, attend palace balls, or walk among their subjects "promoting handicrafts."

The final exhibit is a stiff family grouping of Princess Grace and Prince Rainier and their three young children. The royal family is outfitted in dated seventies fashions that make them look like the Brady Bunch, and the only expression on their faces is a quizzical rictus. And yet, in its artless way, the scene is poignant. Here is the happy home of Their Serene Highnesses, a home still gleaming with fairy dust, magically remote from tragedy and disappointment.

Monaco without Grace Kelly. Ten years after the princess unaccountably lost control of her Rover 3500 on the Moyenne Corniche and sailed past a crash barrier to her death, even the most cynical visitor to Monaco is likely to feel a curious vacancy, the recognition that the principality has been forever sapped of a critical measure of its storybook allure.

The celestial perfection of the royal couple, though, was always something of an illusion. If we can believe her unauthorized biographers, Grace was not a particularly happy princess. She never managed to be comfortable with court folderol or even fully conversant in French. When Rainier asked her in 1966 what she would like for a tenth-anniversary present, she supposedly replied, "A year off." She wanted to act in movies again, but her husband and subjects would not hear of it (Rainier even refused to let her play the Virgin Mary in *King of Kings*), and so she channeled her creative passions into tame pursuits like the promotion of breast-feeding and public performance of light verse. By the last year of her life she was overweight, a bit bibulous, and disinclined to get out of bed in the morning.

To the Monégasque people she is nevertheless a cherished icon. They buried her behind the altar of the cathedral, along with the Grimaldis, the Florestans, the Hippolytes, and many of the other personages on display in the wax museum. Except for the fresh flowers on the marble slab, it would be easy to mistake her tomb for just another medieval resting place. GRATIA PATRICIA, the inscription reads, PRINCIPIS RAINIERII III UXOR.

A few blocks east of the cathedral, towering above the sea cliffs on the south side of the Rock, is the oceanographic museum built by Prince Albert I to showcase his passionate interest in marine biology. The museum is four stories high and from the outside looks like a hall of justice or some other stern government building. Just inside the entrance is a statue of Albert in his yachting cap, and behind him when I visited was a comprehensive exhibit on the marine subject dearest to a Monacan's heart—the natural history and commercial cultivation of pearls.

The museum is an imposing institution and in fact draws more visitors than the Casino, but thanks to the obsessive interests of its creator it has a quirky, personal appeal. We spend an hour or so in the downstairs aquarium, watching the living nautiluses hover motionless in their tanks, and then saunter through a great hall dominated by the sixty-six-foot skeleton of a fin whale that is said to have met its death at the end of Albert's harpoon. The prince's specimens of aquatic life are arrayed along the second-floor gallery walls—hundreds of clear glass tubes in which blanched and wrinkled sea creatures float upended in preservative fluid. I could stay here all day, gazing at lurid abyssal fish and watching films of the mating habits of eels, but it is time to stroll out once again into the glamorous streets, down into the market of La Condamine and up the Boulevard des Moulins, past shops selling chocolate Nativity sets and bristling wild boars made of silver, past uniformed yacht crews on shore leave and jaunty Euro-cads in sweatshirts embossed with heraldic crests. All the young women we pass are beautiful; all the old women are grave. Monte Carlo is so immaculate, so rich, with such an air of being a private estate that my eyes search hungrily for any hint of despair or poor taste. My spirits lift a bit when I notice a purple plush monkey attached by suction cups to the windshield of a Citroen, and I feel a brief frisson of real life when I happen to glance into the first-floor window of an apartment building and see a fat man standing in his underwear, his arms hanging disconsolately at his sides as he stares at a large clock on the opposite wall.

Ah, but it is just as easy to fall into the spirit of the place. For all its hauteur, Monaco is a source of constant whimsy and surprise. Here is a restaurant called Le Texan, with a huge bas-relief of the Alamo behind the bar and tables filled with European diners giving one another puzzled looks as they try to assemble their fajitas. Here are a monumental statue of a woman's breast and, not far away, a fanciful sculpture of Adam and Eve, in which Adam is presented with slicked-back hair and a pencil moustache. And here is Ringo Starr, striding into Rampoldi to take a seat at the table next to ours, his earring glinting in the subdued light.

Now it is the eve of the feast day of Saint Dévote. In the church that was built at the spot where the saint's boat purportedly made landfall, a morning mass is conducted in Monégasque. The sound of the language—an ancient amalgam of French and Italian—is both fluid and percussive. And in the nebulous pleasure ground of Monte Carlo, where nothing seems quite as authentic as it ought to, this elemental speech hits the ear just right, sounding as natural and authoritative as the shriek of an ocean bird. "Santa Dévota," the congregation sings in this strangely comprehensible language, "gardara nostra Roca, aé la proutegerá de tütu má!"

That night a crowd gathers in front of the harbor, where a small fishing boat with a raised sail sits on a bed of palm fronds, ready to be set afire. Every year the Monégasques celebrate the feast of their patron saint by burning a boat, a tradition that originated centuries ago when a fisherman looted the church of Saint Dévote. When the defiler was apprehended and the relics he had stolen were returned, his boat was burned on the beach.

It is Rainier's duty to light the fire, and after a policeman has doused the boat with kerosene a motorcade of black Rolls-Royces punctually arrives. Out of the lead car emerges a portly, elderly man wearing a white muffler and an air of princely fatigue. Rainier is accompanied by his son, Albert, his daughter Caroline, and his grandchildren. Though they are flanked by security guards, they move through the crowd without any sense of urgency or fuss. The public appearance of Rainier in this minute country has a kind of intimacy about it, as if he were the mayor of a village instead of the prince of a realm. Without words or ceremony the royal family torches the boat, and as it is swallowed in greasy flames they repair to a reviewing stand to watch the fireworks over the harbor.

The famous Monte Carlo fireworks are not a disappointment. The sky shimmers with color, and birds circle in frantic confusion. Tendrils of light, falling with 3-D precision from the night sky, are accompanied by rumbling, sputtering blasts that shake the quay on which we are standing and even, I suspect, the ageless monument of the Rock. For some reason, the cadence of the exploding fireworks puts me in mind of the Monégasque rhythms of the morning's mass, and for a moment I have a feeling about where the soul of Monaco resides: somewhere between the legend of Saint Dévote and the fairy tale of Princess Grace, between the natural majesty of the Rock and the architectural frippery of the Casino.

When the fireworks are over, the prince and his family leave the reviewing stand without comment, wearily shake a few hands, and then, to the applause of their subjects, drive off toward the palace. The smell of gunpowder lingers over the quay, and pale, dispersing columns of smoke still hover in the sky. It is 9:00 P.M. The casinos are open, and dawn is years away.

The Anger of Achilles

I wouldn't say it's my favorite painting. That honor—if it is an honor coming from such an untutored critic— would probably fall to some mainstream masterpiece like Vermeer's *The Letter* or Van Gogh's *The Starry Night*. *The Anger of Achilles,* however, stops me in my tracks whenever I go to the Kimbell Art Museum in Fort Worth, and I find I have an affinity for this painting that cuts deeper than textbook appreciation and that continues to surprise me with its strength. When you strike up that kind of relationship with a work of art, it can seem like fate—as if some force is instructing you, for reasons you can't know, to brood over a particular image.

I first saw it a few years ago, when I happened to be in Fort Worth with an afternoon to kill. I was planning to see a matinee of *Raise the Titanic!* but my better self intervened. I could see a lousy movie anytime, but here I was in Fort Worth, and I had never been to the Kimbell. There was a reason for that. I've never been particularly fond of art museums, which have always struck me as too hushed, too decorous. I suppose that, in truth, I have the provincial Texan's deep-seated suspicion of serious culture. As often as not, I feel cowed by art, inadequate and surly. I'm afraid of being taken in, of giving my heart to something that might turn out to be phony, so I tend to hold back, fierce in my ignorance. The museums themselves only reinforce such feelings. In those temples, among the nattering docents and somber, blazer-clad guards, I find myself skulking about like a spy.

But I liked the Kimbell. It was a small place, but it had grandeur too, with its high vaulted ceilings that made the interior seem as lofty and sumptuous as a desert pavilion. Bathed in natural light, imbued with an unforced and appreciative silence, the museum made me feel that I could, for once, let my guard down and just look at the pictures.

The Anger of Achilles was hanging in the southwest gallery then; they've moved it since. I had been making my way along the wall, politely admiring a group of dark and fusty-looking canvases whose subject matter I can no longer remember, when the *Achilles* seized my attention. It was large and bright, and my eyes were drawn to it as if it were a window that had just been thrown open in a gloomy hallway. I liked the painting at first simply because it was easy. It was colorful and clean, with a plain-spoken, unflinching figurative style. It depicted some scene from classical Greek lore, the sort of subject that I usually found to be high-blown and corny. But this work's sincerity was commanding. Four people were compressed within the tight borders of the canvas. On the left was a young warrior in the act of drawing his sword, but something about the languorous contortions of his body, his bland, unreflective face, made this threatening gesture seem unconvincing. The artist, I thought, had failed with this figure, but part of the power of the painting was the way it triumphed over this central flaw. My eyes rested on the faces of the other three characters, faces filled with such sadness and tragic weariness that I was startled by the intensity of my response, by the way I immediately accepted them not as painted forms but as fellow human beings in distress. On the right side of the frame a man—no doubt a king— motioned to the warrior to put down his sword. In the tight confines of the canvas the king's arm appeared a bit foreshortened, but the rest of him was rendered with such confidence and subtlety that matters of technique receded into irrelevance. I simply watched him—the struggle that was apparent in his eyes even as he stared down his antagonist.

Between the king and the warrior stood a young woman with her hands crossed over her chest, her head angled to one side in the moody, otherworldly pose of a Pre-Raphaelite maiden. But there was nothing insipid about her; her sorrowful distraction was authentic. She had passed through some mysterious emotional turbulence, had triumphed over it, and now anchored this scene with her serenity. Behind her, one hand resting comfortingly on her shoulder, stood an older woman— a queen, a mother—her eyes red from crying, looking at the impetuous warrior with sympathy but also with a kind of contempt for the uselessness of his rage.

I wasn't sure exactly what predicament was being portrayed here, and I stared at the painting for quite a while before even thinking to consult the museum label. *The Anger of Achilles,* it said, had been painted in 1819 by Jacques-Louis David. Achilles is the figure on the left, the youth in the act of drawing his sword. The painting presents the moment when he learns that Iphigenia, his betrothed, is to be sacrificed to the goddess Diana instead of married to him. This is all the fault of Agamemnon, the king of the Greeks and the father of Iphigenia. He has killed a deer sacred to Diana and now, when the Greek fleet is massed at Aulis ready to sail against Troy, the angry goddess has turned the wind against it. She will not be appeased unless the daughter of Agamemnon and Clytemnestra is put to death.

Knowing the stakes, I studied the painting again. A scene that could easily have been theatrical and over-wrought was instead almost unbearably calm. Its theme was not so much the heroic clash of wills between gods and men as the mute acceptance of a family tragedy. I was convinced that only a great artist could have made a picture like this, in which the strongest characters were not those who drew their swords in outrage but those who responded with dignity to their own helplessness.

I knew vaguely who David was, but it was not until I consulted an art textbook later that I could recall his other works. He had painted the riveting *Oath of the Horatii* and the gigantic canvas depicting the consecration of Napoleon, both of which hang in the Louvre. And it was David, I realized with some embarrassment at my ignorance, who had created one of the most famous paintings in the world, the portrait of Jean-Paul Marat lying dead in his bathtub.

David painted *The Anger of Achilles* near the end of his life, and thus the painting belongs to a body of work that has been generally dismissed by critics. "Unlike many great artists," states the *Oxford Companion to Art,* "David did not mature with age; his work weakened as the possibility of exerting a moral and social influence receded."

It's true that for most of his life David put his art to passionate use. He was an activist, and he meant for his painting to galvanize and instruct, to figure in the real course of events. He was born in Paris in 1748 and came of age at a time when French taste was beginning to shift away from the pleasant rococo reveries of painters like François Boucher, whose sensual canvases were chockablock with cherubs casting approving looks at pastoral lovers ("Such an inimitable and rare piece of nonsense," Diderot said of one of those paintings).

David admired Boucher, but his soul cried out for something more stringent and consequential. After winning the Prix de Rome and spending several years in Italy brooding over antiquity, he found his niche in "history painting," a genre he infused with the rigorous tenets of Neoclassicism. History painting dealt with noble, ancient scenes. The works were supercharged with moral uplift and bore ponderous titles like *Septimus Severus Reproaching Caracalla for Wishing to Assassinate Him.* In David's hands, history painting was filled with urgent relevance. His *Oath of the Horatii,* which quivers with purpose and commitment, could not be mistaken in its time for anything less than a call to arms for the French Revolution.

In the chaos of that time David rose to dizzying prominence. A self-portrait painted in 1794 shows him unreflective, impatient, his brown eyes blind with fervor. He was a firebrand who embraced the revolution in its full horror and did not flinch. He voted enthusiastically for the execution of King Louis XVI, he cold-bloodedly sketched Marie Antoinette being led to the guillotine, and he served on the Committee for Public Safety, which issued the arrest warrants that led hundreds to their death in the Place de la Revolution. David also threw himself into designing elephantine pageants celebrating the First Republic, in which ornate chariots and revolutionary icons were paraded through the streets and pâpier-maché symbols of monarchy were burned to release flights of doves.

David managed to survive the shifting moods of the revolution, though he narrowly missed going to the guillotine with his denounced friend Robespierre. It was only with the rise of Napoleon that his status and popularity were restored. He flattered the emperor with memorable canvases, including *Bonaparte Crossing the Alps,* which hangs in Versailles, but as Napoleon's court painter he seems to have regarded himself as ill-used and underpaid. When Napoleon fell, David was exiled to Brussels, where he spent the last nine years of his life.

In Brussels in 1819 he painted *The Anger of Achilles.* During his old age he returned to the classical subject matter that had made his reputation, although with the exception of the *Achilles* the subjects themselves were mostly trivial—lounging gods and goddesses and winking cupids that put one in mind of Boucher. With the *Achilles,* David, perhaps for the last time, dealt with themes that were grave and worthy of his troubled experience.

He was offered the chance to go back to Paris, but he chose to stay in Brussels rather than accept the clemency of the monarchy that he despised. "I was old enough to know what I was doing, I didn't act on impulse," he wrote his son about his revolutionary activities. "I can rest here, the years are passing, my conscience is clear, what more do I need?"

The Anger of Achilles was exhibited in Brussels and Ghent. Afterward it was bought by a Parisian collector and kept from public view for more than 150 years. It was acquired by the Newhouse Galleries in New York, which subsequently sold it to the Kimbell in 1980 for a price the museum won't reveal.

When I saw it recently, it was hanging near an exhibit of paintings by Impressionists, who worked in defiance of artists like David and their stalwart meaningfulness. To the Impressionists, a painting like *The Anger of Achilles* must have seemed, for all its undeniable technique, contrived and even comical in its high-minded concerns.

But David was nothing if not high-minded. "It is not only by delighting the eye," he wrote, "that great works of art achieve their purpose, but by making a deep impression, akin to reality, on the mind." By that measure, *The Anger of Achilles* has achieved its purpose, at least with one viewer. It may be a great painting or it may not, but for me it was the painting that took the chill off art, the one that first spoke to me at the moment when I was ready to listen. When I go to the Kimbell now, I no longer feel that museum edginess, because the *Achilles* is there as a touchstone, and my appreciation of it somehow makes me more accepting of the variety of work that surrounds it. But it's to the *Achilles* that I keep returning, marveling at how one of the architects of the Terror could have painted the hurt in Clytemnestra's eyes. Perhaps the impotent Achilles in this picture is in some unconscious way meant to represent David himself, the heedless ideologue who lived long enough to see his zeal reproached and his art booted out of fashion. In his life, David was rash and unthinking, but this painting—an old man's painting—is touched with wisdom. It radiates regret and hard-earned lessons and finally an awful tranquillity.

As I stood in front of it on my last trip, another visitor came up beside me. He was about seventeen, and he towered over my head and seemed as big as a parade float. No doubt he was a guard or tackle on a high school football team, an uneasy combination of muscle and baby fat. He was wearing cowboy boots and Wranglers and a huge bull-rider hat slung low over his eyes. For a long time he stared at the painting, his thumbs hooked behind his belt buckle. Then he said, with an air of wonder and appreciation, "Huh."

Later I saw him in the gift shop, buying a postcard of *The Anger of Achilles* and then slipping it into his breast pocket next to a snuff can. There was an innocence in his response to the painting that I trusted, that made me more confident of my own regard for it. Perhaps what led us both to this painting in the first place was the provincial temperament we shared, the Texan fondness for objects that are direct and weighty and without guile. Of all the paintings in the museum, David's *Achilles* comes the closest to having the common touch. I could imagine the artist tackling some myth closer to our own antiquity—Travis drawing the line at the Alamo, for instance—and creating a weird, powerful hybrid of Neoclassicism and Western art.

"This young man works in the grand manner," Diderot wrote in 1781 when David first exhibited at the French Academy. "He has heart, his faces are expressive without being contrived, the attitudes are noble and natural, he can draw."

What was true in the salons of Paris two hundred years ago is true in Fort Worth today. I thought of David, working in exile in his Brussels studio, his stern mind in repose as the paint touched the canvas. He could not have known that his picture of Achilles would be judged as one of his lesser works, that it would hang in a Texas museum instead of the Louvre. No doubt he would have been disappointed, but he also would have recognized the more important point: that his painting had been true enough, and rigorous enough, to last. The people who admired it now were not the people he had once meant to reach, but he had reached us all the same.

Eighteen Minutes

One summer morning in 1901 a delegation assembled by the Daughters of the Republic of Texas boarded a train at Houston's Grand Central depot and made its way east to the plain of San Jacinto. The battlefield lay, as it does now, on a marshy peninsula where Buffalo Bayou intersected the San Jacinto River. The Houston Ship Channel, neither as grand nor as pestilential as it would later become, had been dredged through the confluence of those two watercourses, and to the eyes of one member of the delegation—a veteran of the battle named J. W. Winters—the bayou must have looked much wider than it had even in that rain-soaked spring of 1836.

Winters would have been eighty-four at the time of the trip—a hawk-faced man with a long white beard cut square across the bottom. He was along to represent the dwindling ranks of the Texas Veterans Association, men who had marched with Sam Houston during the revolution and who found themselves still among the living at the dawn of the new century. They had the pleasure of being referred to, in their lifetimes, as "immortal heroes," and in their reunion photographs they look as stern as gods, their disapproving countenances resting on bushy chin-beards. Every so often one of the veterans would transfix a group of schoolchildren with a first-hand account of that distant April when he had taken part in the charge across the plain of San Jacinto and helped to change the world in the space of eighteen minutes.

When they reached the battlefield Winters took the Daughters and their entourage on a tour, showing them where certain key events had taken place so that those spots could be marked. He first pointed out the place where Santa Anna, the captured Mexican president, had been brought before Houston. S. J. Hendrick, a local judge and chairman of the newly formed San Jacinto Commission, claimed the privilege of placing the first marker, a galvanized cross that had to be driven nine feet into the ground. After his labors, the *Houston Post* wryly noted, "it was observed that he modestly retired and never volunteered thereafter."

A dozen markers were erected that day. In later years the crosses were replaced by granite slabs that look like tombstones. In 1939 the gentle rise at the center of the plain was crowned with a startling apparition. The San Jacinto Monument is a vertical shaft 570 feet high—an emphatic 15 feet taller than the Washington Monument—that ascends with splendid indifference to the flat coastal prairie surrounding it. Topped by a giant stone star, its base covered with heroic friezes, the monument makes a statement that is not historical but religious: here God saw fit to create Texas.

The monument was intended as a grand, solitary stroke, a building that would command the eye on that flat horizon like a bolt of lightning. But when you approach the San Jacinto Battleground State Historical Park today—150 years after the battle—this gleaming temple to Texas liberty is the last thing you notice. Its place in the skyline is crowded out by refinery towers and dense columns of vapor that drift vertically across the landscape. Everything is dreary and fetid, rich with the atmosphere of industrial gloom. Yet the battlefield itself is vibrant. Unlike the Alamo, which can seem as remote and mysterious as Stonehenge, San Jacinto has few secrets. Its history lies close at hand.

In 1836 the storied plain of San Jacinto was merely a pasture belonging to a widow named Peggy McCormick. The land took its name from the river, which according to one story had been discovered by Spanish explorers on the feast day of Saint Hyacinth of Cracow, a Dominican missionary. It was the chaos of the Texas Revolution that turned Mrs. McCormick's grazing land into strategic ground.

After the fall of the Alamo and the massacre at Goliad, Houston led the remnant of the Texas army eastward across the Colorado and the Brazos, buying time as he searched for any possible advantage to use against the superior Mexican forces. He found his luck at San Jacinto, where Santa Anna, hoping to cut off Houston's retreat, positioned his army with its back to the water only a mile or so away from Houston's camp under the live oaks. "Any youngster would have done better," wrote Pedro Delgado, a Mexican officer, who was convinced by that time that Santa Anna was a raving lunatic.

Thanks to the information provided by the exemplary scout Deaf Smith, Houston was made aware of just how unfortunate Santa Anna's position was. More than 900 Texans were filled with hatred and vengeance and the sure knowledge that if they failed, everything was lost. On the other side of the plain were 1,200 homesick troops, weary of an endless campaign in the hellish Mexican sub-province of Texas. Santa Anna knew the Texans were nearby, but he apparently never realized the size of the force. He was stunningly overconfident and maybe a little hazy from opium abuse. Though his soldiers skirmished with the rebels on April 20, Santa Anna made only perfunctory efforts to safeguard his camp against assault. Certainly he set no great standard of vigilance. On the afternoon of the twenty-first, when the attack came, he was in his luxurious three-room tent where, according to legend, he was entertaining a mulatto servant girl who would henceforth be known as the Yellow Rose of Texas.

It was not so much a battle as a massacre. The Texans set out on foot in a long file across the plain. Since it suited Sam Houston's magnificent temperament to make himself as big a target as possible, he rode before his men on a white horse named Saracen. The cavalry, led by a Georgia poet named Mirabeau B. Lamar, was on the right flank, cutting off the enemy's only landward escape route.

A slight ridge in the middle of the plain helped to conceal the Texans until they were practically at the

Mexican breastworks. Before Santa Anna's men could unstack their rifles, they were being torn apart by horseshoes and scrap metal fired from a pair of cannons called the Twin Sisters, a gift to the rebels from the citizens of Cincinnati. The Mexicans were routed. It was Houston who reported that the battle lasted eighteen minutes, and in terms of any formal military operations, he was probably correct. But the slaughter went on all that evening and for several days thereafter.

Santa Anna escaped the battlefield, but was run to ground the next day. He was in disguise, wearing clothes he had found in the abandoned slave quarters of a nearby ranch. Apparently he didn't have the heart to conceal himself entirely, because under his ragged jacket he was wearing a shirt with diamond studs.

J. W. Winters was digging graves for the eight men killed on the Texan side when Santa Anna was brought into camp. "Some called out, 'Shoot him! Hang him!'" Winters remembered, but Houston, lying beneath a big tree, in pain from an ankle wound, ordered the agitators removed. Three other Mexican divisions were scouring Texas, and Houston was shrewd enough to know that his victory would be short-lived unless he could bargain with Santa Anna's life. The two leaders had some testy words about the Alamo and Goliad, but all in all Houston seemed to have been a good host. Santa Anna, he recognized, was not just a vanquished foe. Craven and demeaned as he appeared, he was still Houston's kindred spirit—a man with an uncomplicated belief in his own grandeur. For Houston and Santa Anna, the battle of San Jacinto was a pageant. For the rest of the world, it was history.

Despite the immense changes of the past century and a half, the contours of San Jacinto have remained essentially the same. At one end of the battlefield you can still find the trees—or their descendants—where the Texans camped; at the other you can still see the slough that cut off the Mexican retreat. The swell in the middle of the field that was so critical in concealing the rebel advance is still detectable, though from the ground it is hard to register anything but the spectacle of the monument soaring overhead.

Just beneath the huge four-sided star that crowns the monument is an observation platform. From that vantage point you can look out over the battlefield and across the Houston Ship Channel. If it's a relatively clear day the air will be hazy, but the sun will be bright on the grillwork and storage tanks of the plants. The water in the reflecting pool below the monument is as dark as a shadow and reflects nothing, but it guides the eye portentously to the Texan end of the battlefield. From the semicircular cockpit of the observation platform, the Mexican side of the field is pointedly not visible.

At the base of the tower is an excellent museum, filled with yellowing letters and dispatches, with popinjay uniforms and Brown Bess muskets. In one display case is Houston's famous ring, a thin gold band with the word "Honor" inscribed inside. Next to it is Houston's dictionary, opened to show the place where he had rashly crossed out the word "temporize" and written in the margin "out with it!" The two objects sum up Houston neatly enough. Though he was ruled by a theatrical personality, his innermost sentiments were nonetheless grave and earnest. He was the perfect leader for his rebel army, a man of intrigue and sweeping gestures. As governor of Tennessee he had created a wonderful scandal when a few months after his marriage his bride mysteriously ran home to her parents. Houston refused to give a hint about what had gone wrong between them, and he offered to kill anyone who might stain Mrs. Houston's honor by speculating. In disgrace, he resigned the governorship and ended up in Texas after living some years with the Cherokees in Oklahoma, who knew him affectionately as "Big Drunk."

Like Houston, a good percentage of his men had come to Texas to escape disgrace or prosecution, or to steal land from Mexico and fulfill their own personal visions of manifest destiny. Some were mere criminals; others were high-born and florid, true to the romantic timbre of the age. In this latter category were such gentlemen as the versifying Lamar, or John M. Allen, who'd been with Lord Byron at Missolonghi, or Robert Potter, the Republic's Secretary of the Navy, whose offended honor had caused him to castrate personally two men he suspected of having relations with his wife.

The Texans' cause was not nearly as just as it was inevitable. They simply wanted Texas more than Mexico did, and they were willing to take it. The fact that Santa Anna was a true tyrant only helped to make the Texans' rhetoric of "liberty" and "freedom" all the more plausible. The Mexican president was, in many ways, a marvel: He was a cruel man upon whom fortune shone. As a despot, he was almost comically irrepressible, a bad penny. By the time he died, in 1876, he had been president of Mexico eleven times. In the spring of 1836 he was at the peak of his peculiar form—a sybarite leading an army into the wilderness, unconcerned with the hardships he was inflicting upon his men and so uninformed about the local geography that he thought the rain-swollen streams he encountered were the result of melting snow from nearby mountain ranges.

Anglo Texans have always regarded Santa Anna with

contempt, and nowhere is this attitude more apparent than at San Jacinto. The Texan side of the battlefield has been fitted out with every sort of commemorative trapping—plaques, walkways, statues, replicas of the Twin Sisters, a sundial, and an elaborate grave marker honoring the Texans who died as a result of the battle. "We have read of deeds of chivalry," the inscription on this marker proclaims, "and perused with ardor the annals of war; we have contemplated, with the highest emotions of sublimity, the loud roaring thunder, the desolating tornado, and the withering simoom of the desert; but neither of these, nor all, inspired us with emotions like those felt on this occasion."

No such lofty sentiments decorate the Mexican side of San Jacinto, and no gravestone marks the 630 dead soldiers the Texans left to rot on the field with their pockets rifled and sometimes their scalps removed. Here and there granite markers indicate the placement of troops, but it's clear that the intent of the park is not to interpret the battle but to glory in its consequences. Where the Mexicans were slaughtered, one finds only picnic tables. The Texans to this day have not been gracious in victory, and a trip to the battlefield does little to dispel the suspicion that the Texas Revolution, for all its airs, was in its darkest aspects a mean little race war.

The slough that cut off the Mexican retreat is now named for Santa Anna. Its shallow waters are dark and uninviting. Houston's men, in their killing fever, stood at its bank shooting Mexicans until it was so filled with the dead that it was possible to walk across it. Probably they and their effects are still there, buried in the mud.

Houston tried to stop the carnage. "Gentlemen! Gentlemen! Gentlemen!" he cried futilely from his horse. Other

Texans acted, sometimes heroically, to save the Mexicans from the wrath of their comrades, but the Texans had a lot of pent-up fury to spend. "Can such wicked men exist?" Delgado asked himself. He was lucky enough to be taken alive, but during the next few nights under guard in the enemy camp he and the other prisoners lived in almost constant fear of being shot in retaliation for the Alamo or Goliad. At one point, watching their captors build a bonfire, the Mexicans were sure they were about to be burned alive.

The Texans were overwrought with victory and the nagging fear that the rest of the Mexican forces might yet decide to attack. As they grew more secure, so did their prisoners, but the field of San Jacinto was still littered with corpses and at night the Mexicans heard the howling and barking of wolves as they fought over the remains.

But those ghoulish sounds are far distant now. San Jacinto, as the monument insistently reminds us, was a triumph: the sixteenth most important battle in history, according to one historian. In those few critical minutes the winner took all. Mexican Texas ceased to exist the moment one of Santa Anna's generals received a letter from El Presidente detailing "an unfortunate encounter yesterday afternoon."

Santa Anna was sent back to Mexico by way of Washington, where he was entertained by President Jackson. Most of the rest of his army was taken by steamer to Galveston, where they languished awhile before being allowed to return home. Peggy McCormick repeatedly appealed to the Republic of Texas to clean up her cow pasture, but the dead Mexicans lay there all summer long, their bones scattered or eaten by scavengers.

Mexican Texas was gone, but 150 astonishing years lay

ahead for the nation and the nation-state that replaced it. It was the old veterans like J. W. Winters who lived to see the impact of San Jacinto more clearly than anyone. In the years ahead they stood by, honored ghosts at San Jacinto Day festivities, watching the parades and bicycle races and listening to open-air concerts by such groups as Professor Herb's Light Guard Band.

"Comrades," one of the veterans lamented on April 21, 1897, "our ranks are thinning fast." In 1907, before nature could do it for them, the Texas Veterans mustered themselves out of service in a ceremony at Austin's Driskill Hotel. Winters died in 1903. The last of them to go was Alfonzo Steele. He had been a teenager at the time of the battle and had been seriously wounded in the assault. In later years he recounted how, though woozy from loss of blood, he had managed to raise his rifle and drop a Mexican who was trying to surrender. Steele was ninety-four when he died in his sleep. "Thus," reported the newspaper, "did this old Texas veteran cheerfully bid his family 'good night' to bid his old San Jacinto comrades 'good morning' on the morrow."

Rock and Sky

We know the Anasazi, to the degree that we can ever know them, by what they left behind. The rock walls of the Southwest are still adorned with their fading art: whirling circles, handprints, owl-faced figures. On mesa tops and along canyon trails, the ground underfoot is strewn with thin gray fragments of their pottery. And of course there are the ruins, those shrines to fleeting civilizations and to the permanence of the American landscape.

At Mesa Verde National Park, which includes the most famous of the Anasazi sites, most of the best-known ruins are cliff villages, secreted away beneath the brow of the mesa in crevices that open out onto the deep canyons and distant plains of southwestern Colorado. From afar, these tidy dwellings with their weathered masonry are barely discernible from the vaulting cliff faces surrounding them. Chinked tight against the contours of the rock, they look like giant mud-dauber nests. They have an air of camouflage, of natural mimicry, that seems like a deliberate aesthetic, something the inhabitants took pains to achieve. Looking across the canyons at these villages, nestled and disguised beneath their sandstone overhangs, you feel they were never meant to be discovered.

But of course they were discovered. Here, in the least-visited public section of Mesa Verde, on a day with steady rain falling and no hope of sunshine, the cliff dwellings were overrun by visitors who had come to view the haunted remains of the Anasazi culture. Leaving the train, my wife and I and our three kids descended to the ruins on paved footpaths, passing below the alcoves of nesting ravens and the shallow indentations in the cliff face that the Anasazi used as hand- and footholds for their precipitous travels to the canyon floor. Some of the tourists stopped at each numbered marker to consult diligently their interpretive trail guides; others merely took in the ruins with a quick sweep of their video cameras and hustled out of the rain. All in all, we were the usual unholy horde of sightseers, trying to absorb at a glance what we should have let seep into our bones. But I felt we were doing no harm. Like the other Anasazi sites I had visited in the last few weeks, this place seemed enclosed in a protective bubble of solitude—self-regarding, unyielding, serene.

The Anasazi left behind literally thousands of such places, scattered throughout the desert washes, canyons, and mesa tops of the Colorado Plateau. They are the best-known unknown people of ancient America. The Anasazi are whom we have in mind when we speak vaguely of "cliff dwellers," that long-ago culture that lived in a universe bounded by rock and sky.

The heart of their civilization lay in what is known today as the Four Corners, where Colorado, Utah, New Mexico, and Arizona come together in a universe of cloud-swept plains and eerie land forms. The ancient magic of this country is a lodestone for travelers. Along the freeways and washboard roads we must have seen three hundred vehicles just like ours—Dodge Caravans crowned with plastic cartop carriers from Sears; children with Walkman headphones staring out the window at moody spires of rock, at Navajo dogs herding their sheep toward the brushy shelter of a summer hogan. There were streams of RV's with the owners' names hospitably written beneath the window or on the spare-tire covers— "The Rudloes," "The Pinckneys," "Hi, We're the Guthries." And there were buses crammed with Italian, Austrian, or Belgian passengers, with Navajo drivers at the wheel. Like us, they were all on the Anasazi tour. They had come to see firsthand these mysterious habitations that suggested an America not just from another time but from another realm of human perception.

The Anasazi's claim on our imagination rests largely on the popular notion of them as "the Indians who disappeared." Their intriguing little cities were already long abandoned when the Navajo filtered down from the mountains in the fifteenth century. The Navajo called the vanished residents by a word that, after centuries of being garbled in the polyglot Southwest, comes down to us as "Anasazi." The original word meant either "the ancient ones" or "the enemies of our ancient ones." But exactly who the Anasazi had been—or what they called themselves—was as much a mystery to the newly arrived Navajo as it is to us.

The archaeological record, rich as it is, gives us only a blinkered understanding of Anasazi life. We have the sense of an industrious, questing people whose world hummed with spiritual energy. The Anasazi built not only cities but roads as well—hundreds of miles of broad thoroughfares that can still be traced across the desert floor. They built underground chambers, sometimes connected by secret passageways to looming castle towers. To provide water to their fields, they constructed a system of irrigation canals, dams, and reservoirs. They wove cotton and made blankets from the feathers of their domesticated turkeys. Journeying to the south, perhaps all the way to the moody, glittering cultures of the Valley of Mexico, they came back enriched with trade goods and knowledge of agriculture. They brought back macaws and tried to keep them as pets, but the jungle birds did not survive in the arid Anasazi country, and when they died they were sometimes buried as lords.

What happened to the Anasazi? That is the great riddle. Were they driven out by enemies? Did their crops fail? Did their political structure break down? Were they abducted by UFO's? No one knows for sure, but the question is not quite as unanswerable as popular lore suggests. The Anasazi, along with their contemporaries in the Southwest—the Sinagua, the Hohokam, the Mogollon—were hunter-gatherers who had evolved into an agricultural society in a part of the world where water was scarce, growing seasons short, and crucial resources finite. As their population grew, they harvested more and more timber for roof beams, cleared more and more land for farm plots. Erosion became a problem, and drought, and then a sudden climatic change in the late thirteenth century brought on longer winters. At some point, it appears, they just decided to move along.

The Anasazi did not exactly disappear off the face of the earth. The majority of them migrated east and south to the banks of the Rio Grande and helped create the various Pueblo cultures that are still vital today. Others moved into Arizona, settling around Black Mesa and contributing to the ancestry of the Hopis. But the legend endures that somehow they were simply winked out of existence, leaving nothing behind but their strange dwellings and the restive spirits that still haunt them.

For anyone with any imagination, it is difficult to prowl among these ruins with an entirely clear head. They do have an irresistible, otherworldly charge. Partly this comes from their natural surroundings. The cliffs of Canyon de Chelly, with their whorled and sweeping expanses of rock, seem to be the fossilized record of a transitory event, like a powerful wind or a surging sea. The broad desert corridor of Chaco Canyon is a more subtle landscape, unremarkable at first sight, but it absorbs and reflects sunlight in ways that can make it seem spectral or even, to certain receptive minds, holy. Then there are the great tabletops of Mesa Verde, which rise in the blue distance like icebergs looming on a flat ocean, or the gaping overhangs, bigger than the Hollywood Bowl, that house the old cities of Betatakin or Keet Seel.

You see these places, and you have an immediate regard for the people who chose to live in them. Whoever the Anasazi were, whatever their pragmatic needs for food and shelter and arable land, they seem to have picked the sites for their houses and cities out of a craving for physical beauty and intimate contact with the landscape. They did not impose. Their residences took the forms that the natural surroundings suggested—built into crevices, bundled up against cliffs, dug into the earth, or carved discreetly into the rock itself. The Anasazi were not ecological saints—they wore out the land in places and stripped it of its resources—but they were attuned to the raw presence of the earth in ways that do not seem possible anymore.

One day when there was a driving rain and the dirt road to Hovenweep National Monument had closed, we pulled up at the Anasazi Heritage Center, near Cortez, Colorado, and browsed among the exhibits for an hour or two until the sky began to clear. The children marveled at a holographic bust of an Anasazi man. When they looked at it from one angle it was a bare skull; from another, a handsome, vacant face. If they shifted their eyes in the slightest, however, the two images came together, so that the man's face and skull appeared as overlapping, transparent clouds. It was like a taunt, a pestering reminder of how distant and unreachable the Anasazi would always be.

But as I looked at the other exhibits, I felt the gap begin to shrink. Anasazi handicrafts are contemporary, if only in the sense that they are timeless. I was drawn to the stately gray or russet surfaces of the pottery, streaked and crosshatched with soft black lines; and to an unforgettable frog pendant, carved out of three thin strips of overlaid shell, decorated with bulging turquoise eyes. One corner of the museum was devoted to a full-scale model of a pit house. This was the sort of dwelling the Anasazi lived in until about A.D. 900 or so, when they began building their houses above ground, on their way to creating the multistoried apartment cities that are their most imposing relics. What struck me about this pit house was how deep it was set into the earth and how secretive and snug it appeared, down to the entrance tunnel that resembled nothing so much as the entrance to an animal burrow.

Even after they began to build their houses on the edge of the sky, the Anasazi still indulged a cultural yearning to be underground. Their pit houses lived on in the form of kivas, the ceremonial cellars that underlay the court-yards of almost every village. In the kivas the Anasazi conducted their rituals, held clan gatherings, and re-flected on the foggy times when their ancestors had climbed out of the Lower World through a hole in the sky and emerged here, onto the deserts and mesas of the Fourth World.

In Pueblo Bonito, the largest of the structures in Chaco Canyon, we walked in the late afternoon among the ruins of the courtyard. There were kivas everywhere, unroofed and unexcavated, so that the courtyard re-sembled a moon surface pitted with meteor craters. Except for the missing roofs, every feature of the kivas was still visible—the hearths and draft deflectors, the benches and pilasters lining the curved walls, the niches that once held sacred paraphernalia. In the floor of each kiva was a shallow round hole known as a *sipapu* (or *sipapuni*), which commemorated the Place of Emer-gence, the opening through which the ancestors first appeared from below. In Hopi mythology, which pre-sumably echoes the events of the Anasazi creation story, the ancestors sent a scout up into the Fourth World in the form of a catbird they had fashioned from clay and magically coaxed into life. When the catbird reported back favorably, the humans climbed up from the Lower

World on a bamboo stalk, and when they had all passed through the *sipapu,* they covered the hole with water.

"Remember the *sipapuni,*" these Anasazi pioneers were told by Spider Grandmother, the messenger of the Sun Spirit, "for you will not see it again. You will go on long migrations. You will build villages and abandon them for new migrations. Wherever you stop to rest, leave your marks on the rocks and cliffs so that others will know who was there before them."

The Anasazi did as they were instructed, marking the rocks, building their towns, and then, when it was time, drifting away. But they were not nomads, and you can see in the ruins they left behind an expectation of permanence, as if the builders of these cities believed they had arrived not at a way station but at a journey's end. The construction of Pueblo Bonito alone required, according to one estimate, over a million dressed stones. And the city today—ruined and sagging as it is—looks no more transient than the fractured cliffs that rise behind it.

The children scrambled ahead of us as we wandered through the interior spaces of Pueblo Bonito, their voices growing fainter as they progressed through a bewildering maze of rooms. The doors were low to the ground and shaped like capital T's, the walls cool and stout. Where ceilings survived, the small rooms were as dark as medieval cloisters, but most of the time these two- and three-story buildings were open to the sky, their floors marked by beams of piñon pine still bearing the scars of stone axes. I stopped and tried to call to mind the life of this place—to visualize these small, smoke-darkened rooms in the dead of winter, the sound of human conversation in an unknown language, the guttural mutterings of turkeys, the barking of dogs, the noises of chipping, flaking, grinding, the creaking of looms, the snapping of piñon fires, the hypnotic drone of a singer's voice rising from the ventilation shaft of a kiva.

But seven centuries of silence were too powerful an obstacle for my imagination to penetrate, and after a while I gave up and walked across the park road and climbed down into a huge kiva known as Casa Riconada. The kiva was almost seventy feet across, and without the roof that had once covered its hearths and banquette it looked like a miniature sports arena or an ancient Roman bath whose waters had long since ceased to flow. I took a seat on the bench and experienced a vague, religious twinge, feeling observed from above, as if this empty kiva served to focus the eye of God.

The Anasazi would not have thought of it that way. In their time this kiva would have been covered with a lattice of wooden beams, its roof paved with field stones, its sacred space enclosed in shadow. They would have looked not up to the sky, but down to the floor, to the *sipapu* from which their ancestors had first entered the Fourth World.

The Fourth World isn't what it used to be, now that it's overrun with vacationing families like my own, searching simultaneously for revelation and a vacant room in the nearest Motel 6. But in spots, in these crumbling walls and kivas that have yet to be deconsecrated by time or abuse, it must be close to the world that the Anasazi beheld. We sit in these ruins and try to invoke them—try to grasp who they were and why we feel their absence so sharply—even as they continue to disappear, climbing up their bamboo stalk to the next hole in the sky.

"The Tiger Is God"

When tigers attack men, they do so in a characteristic way. They come from behind, from the right side, and when they lunge it is with the intent of snapping the neck of the prey in their jaws. Most tiger victims die swiftly, their necks broken, their spinal cords compressed or severed high up on the vertebral column.

Ricardo Tovar, a fifty-nine-year-old keeper at the Houston Zoo, was killed by a tiger on May 12, 1988. The primary cause of death was a broken neck, although most of the ribs on the left side of his chest were fractured as well, and there were multiple lacerations on his face and right arm. No one witnessed the attack, and no one would ever know exactly how and why it took place, but the central nightmarish event was clear. Tovar had been standing at a steel door separating the zookeepers' area from the naturalistic tiger display outside. Set into the door was a small viewing window—only slightly larger than an average television screen—made of wire-reinforced glass. Somehow the tiger had broken the glass, grabbed the keeper, and pulled him through the window to his death.

Fatal zoo accidents occur more frequently than most people realize. The year before Tovar died, a keeper in the Fort Worth Zoo was crushed by an elephant, and in 1985, an employee of the Bronx Zoo was killed by two Siberian tigers—the same subspecies as the one that attacked Tovar—when she mistakenly entered the tiger display while the animals were still there. But there was something especially haunting about the Houston incident, something that people could not get out of their minds. It had to do with the realization of a fear built deep into our genetic code: the fear that a beast could appear out of nowhere—through a window!—and snatch us away.

The tiger's name was Miguel. He was eleven years old—middle-aged for a tiger—and had been born at the Houston Zoo to a mother who was a wild-caught Siberian. Siberians are larger in size than any of the other subspecies, and their coats are heavier. Fewer than three hundred of them are now left in the frozen river valleys and hardwood forests of the Soviet Far East, though they were once so plentiful in that region that Cossack troops were sent in during the construction of the Trans-Baikal railway specifically to protect the workers from tiger attacks. Miguel was of mixed blood—his father was a zoo-reared Bengal—but his Siberian lineage was dominant. He was a massive 450-pound creature whose disposition had been snarly ever since he was a cub. Some of the other tigers at the zoo were as placid and affectionate as house cats, but Miguel filled his keepers with caution. Oscar Mendietta, a keeper who retired a few weeks before Tovar's death, remembers the way Miguel would sometimes lunge at zoo personnel as they walked by his holding cage, his claws unsheathed and protruding through the steel mesh. "He had," Mendietta says, "an intent to kill."

Tovar was well aware of Miguel's temperament. He had been working with big cats in the Houston Zoo since 1982, and his fellow keepers regarded him as a cautious and responsible man. Like many old-time zookeepers, he was a civil servant with no formal training in zoology, but he had worked around captive animals most of his life (before coming to Houston, he had been a keeper at the San Antonio Zoo) and had gained a good deal of practical knowledge about their behavior. No one regarded Miguel's aggressiveness as aberrant. Tovar and the other keepers well understood the fact that tigers were supposed to be dangerous.

In 1987 the tigers and other cats had been moved from their outdated display cages to brand-new facilities with outdoor exhibit areas built to mimic the animals' natural environments. The Siberian tiger exhibit—in a structure known as the Phase II building—comprised about a quarter of an acre. It was a wide rectangular space decorated with shrubs and trees, a few fake boulders, and a water-filled moat. The exhibit's backdrop was a depiction, in plaster and cement, of a high rock wall seamed with stress fractures.

Built into the wall, out of public view, was a long corridor lined with the cats' holding cages, where the tigers were fed and confined while the keepers went out into the display to shovel excrement and hose down the area. Miguel and the other male Siberian, Rambo, each had a holding cage, and they alternated in the use of the outdoor habitat, since two male tigers occupying the same space guaranteed monumental discord. Next to Rambo's cage was a narrow alcove through which the keepers went back and forth from the corridor into the display. The alcove was guarded by two doors. The one with the viewing window led outside. Another door, made of steel mesh, closed off the interior corridor.

May 12 was a Thursday. Tovar came to work at about six-thirty in the morning, and at that hour he was alone. Rambo was secure in his holding cage and Miguel was outside—it had been his turn that night to have the run of the display.

Thursdays and Sundays were "fast" days. Normally the tigers were fed a daily ration of ten to fifteen pounds of ground fetal calf, but twice a week their food was withheld in order to keep them from growing obese in confinement. The animals knew which days were fast days, and on those mornings they were sometimes balky about coming inside, since no food was being offered. Nevertheless, the tigers had to be secured in their holding cages while the keepers went outside to clean the display. On this morning, Tovar had apparently gone to the viewing window to check the whereabouts of Miguel when the tiger did not come inside, even though the keepers usually made a point of not entering the alcove until they were certain that both animals were locked up in their holding cages. The viewing window was so small and the habitat itself so panoramic that the chances of spotting the tiger from the window were slim. Several of the keepers had wondered why there was a window there at all, since it was almost useless as an observation post and since one would never go through the door in the first place without being certain that the tigers were in their cages.

But that was where Tovar had been, standing at a steel door with a panel of reinforced glass, when the tiger attacked. John Gilbert, the senior zookeeper who supervised the cat section, stopped in at the Phase II building a little after seven-thirty, planning to discuss with Tovar the scheduled sedation of a lion. He had just entered the corridor when he saw broken glass on the floor outside the steel mesh door that led to the alcove. The door was unlocked—it had been opened by Tovar when he entered the alcove to look out the window. Looking through the mesh, Gilbert saw the shards of glass hanging from the window frame and Tovar's cap, watch, and a single rubber boot lying on the floor. Knowing something dreadful had happened, he called Tovar's name, then pushed on the door and cautiously started to enter the alcove. He was only a few paces away from the broken window when the tiger's head suddenly appeared there, filling its jagged frame. His heart pounding, Gilbert backed off, slammed and locked the mesh door behind him and radioed for help.

Tom Dieckow, a wiry, white-bearded Marine veteran of the Korean War, was the zoo's exhibits curator. He was also in charge of its shooting team, a seldom-convened body whose task was to kill, if necessary, any escaped zoo animal that posed an immediate threat to the public. Dieckow was in his office in the service complex building when he heard Gilbert's emergency call. He grabbed a twelve-gauge shotgun, commandeered an electrician's pickup truck, and arrived at the tiger exhibit two minutes later. He went around to the front of the habitat and saw Miguel standing there, calm and unconcerned, with Tovar's motionless body lying face down fifteen feet away. Dieckow did not shoot. It was his clear impression that the keeper was dead, that the harm was already done. By that time the zoo's response team had gathered outside the exhibit. Miguel stared at the onlookers and then picked up Tovar's head in his jaws and started to drag him off.

"I think probably what crossed that cat's mind at that point," Dieckow speculated later, "is 'look at all those scavengers across there that are after my prey. I'm gonna move it.' He was just being a tiger."

Dieckow raised his shotgun again, this time with the intention of shooting Miguel, but because of all the brush and ersatz boulders in the habitat, he could not get a clear shot. He fired into the water instead, causing the startled tiger to drop the keeper, and then fired twice more as another zoo worker discharged a fire extinguisher from the top of the rock wall. The commotion worked, and Miguel retreated into his holding cage.

The Houston Zoo opened a half-hour late that day. Miguel and all the other big cats were kept inside until zoo officials could determine if it was safe—both for the cats and for the public—to exhibit them again. For a few days the zoo switchboard was jammed with calls from people wanting to express their opinion on whether the tiger should live or die. But for the people at the zoo that issue had never been in doubt.

"It's automatic with us," John Werler, the zoo director, told me when I visited his office a week after the incident. "To what end would we destroy the tiger? If we followed this argument to its logical conclusion, we'd have to destroy every dangerous animal in the zoo collection."

Werler was a reflective, kindly looking man who was obviously weighed down by a load of unpleasant concerns. There was the overall question of zoo safety, the specter of lawsuits, and most recently the public anger of a number of zoo staffers who blamed Tovar's death on the budget cuts, staffing shortages, and bureaucratic indifference that forced keepers to work alone in potentially dangerous environments. But the dominant mood of the zoo, the day I was there, appeared to be one of simple sadness and shock.

"What a terrible loss," read a sympathy card from the staff of the Fort Worth Zoo that was displayed on a coffee table. "May you gain strength and support to get you through this awful time."

The details of the attack were still hazy, and still eerie to think about. Unquestionably, the glass door panel had not been strong enough, but exactly how Miguel had broken it, how he had killed Tovar—and why—remained the subjects of numb speculation. One point was beyond dispute: A tiger is a predator, its mission on the earth is to kill, and in doing so it often displays awesome strength and dexterity.

An Indian researcher, using live deer and buffalo calves as bait, found that the elapsed time between a tiger's secure grip on the animal's neck and the prey's subsequent death was anywhere from thirty-five to ninety seconds. In other circumstances the cat will not choose to be so swift. Sometimes a tiger will kill an elephant calf by snapping its trunk and waiting for it to bleed to death, and it is capable of dragging the carcass in its jaws for miles. (A full-grown tiger possesses the traction power of thirty men.) When a mother tiger is teaching her cubs to hunt, she might move in on a calf, cripple it with a powerful bite to its rear leg, and stand back and let the cubs practice on the helpless animal.

Tigers have four long canine teeth—fangs. The two in the upper jaw are tapered along the sides to a shearing edge. Fourteen of the teeth are molars, for chewing meat and grinding bone. Like other members of the cat family, tigers have keen, night-seeing eyes, and their hearing is so acute that Indonesian hunters—convinced that a tiger could hear the wind whistling through a man's nose hairs—always kept their nostrils carefully barbered. The pads on the bottom of a tiger's paws are surprisingly sensitive, easily blistered or cut on hot, prickly terrain. But the claws within, five on each front paw and four in the hind paws, are protected like knives in an upholstered box.

They are not idle predators; when they kill, they kill to eat. Even a well-fed tiger in a zoo keeps his vestigial repertoire of hunting behaviors intact. (Captive breeding programs, in fact, make a point of selecting in favor of aggressive predatory behavior, since the ultimate hope of these programs is to bolster the dangerously low stock of free-living tigers.) In the zoo, tigers will stalk birds that land in their habitats, and they grow more alert than most people would care to realize when children pass before their gaze. Though stories of man-eating tigers have been extravagantly embellished over the centuries, the existence of such creatures is not legendary. In the Sunderbans, the vast delta region that spans the border of India and Bangladesh, more than four hundred people have been killed by tigers in the last decade. So many fishermen and honey collectors have been carried off that a few years ago officials at the Sunderbans tiger preserve began stationing electrified dummies around the park to encourage the tigers to seek other prey. One percent of all tigers, according to a German biologist who studied them in the Sunderbans, are "dedicated" man-eaters: When they go out hunting, they're after people. Up to a third of all tigers will kill and eat a human if they come across one, though they don't make a special effort to do so.

It is not likely that Miguel attacked Ricardo Tovar out of hunger. Except for the killing wounds inflicted by the tiger, the keeper's body was undisturbed. Perhaps something about Tovar's movements on the other side of the window intrigued the cat enough to make him spring, a powerful lunge that sent him crashing through the glass. Most likely the tiger was surprised, and frightened, and reacted instinctively. There is no evidence that he came all the way through the window. Probably he just grabbed Tovar by the chest with one paw, crushed him against the steel door, and with unthinkable strength pulled him through the window and killed him outside.

John Gilbert, the senior keeper who had been the first on the scene that morning, took me inside the Phase II building to show me where the attack had taken place. Gilbert was a sandy-haired man in his thirties, still shaken and subdued by what he had seen. His recitation of the events was as formal and precise as that of a witness at an inquest.

"When I got to this point," Gilbert said as we passed through the security doors that led to the keepers' corridor, "I saw the broken glass on the floor. I immediately yelled Mr. Tovar's name . . ."

The alcove in which Tovar had been standing was much smaller than I had pictured it, and seeing it first-hand made one thing readily apparent: it was a trap. Its yellow cinder-block walls were no more than four feet apart. The ceiling was made of steel mesh and a door of the same material guarded the exit to the corridor. The space was so confined it was not difficult to imagine—it was impossible *not* to imagine—how the tiger had been able to catch Tovar by surprise with a deadly swipe from his paw.

And there was the window. Covered with a steel plate now, its meager dimensions were still visible. The idea of being hauled through that tiny space by a tiger had an almost supernatural resonance—as if the window were a portal through which mankind's most primeval terrors were allowed to pass unobstructed.

Gilbert led me down the corridor. We passed the holding cage of Rambo, who hung his head low and let out a grumbling basso roar so deep it sounded like a tremor in the earth. Then we were standing in front of Miguel.

"Here he is," Gilbert said, looking at the animal with an expression on his face that betrayed a sad welter of emotions. "He's quite passive right now."

The tiger was reclining on the floor, looking at us without concern. I noticed his head, which seemed to me wider than the window he had broken out. His eyes were yellow, and when the great head pivoted in my direction and Miguel's eyes met mine I looked away reflexively, afraid of their hypnotic gravity. The tiger stood up and began to pace, his gigantic pads treading noiselessly on the concrete. The bramble of black stripes that decorated his head was as neatly symmetrical as a Rorschach inkblot, and his orange fur—conceived by evolution as camouflage—was a florid, provocative presence in the featureless confines of the cage.

Miguel idly pawed the steel guillotine door that covered the entrance to his cage, and then all of a sudden he reared on his hind legs. I jumped back a little, startled and dwarfed. The top of Miguel's head nestled against the ceiling mesh of his cage, his paws were spread to either side. In one silent moment, his size and scale seemed to have increased exponentially. He looked down at Gilbert and me. In Miguel's mind, I suspected, his keeper's death was merely a vignette, a mostly forgotten moment of fright and commotion that had intruded one day upon the tiger's torpid existence in the zoo. But it was hard not to look up at that immense animal and read his posture as a deliberate demonstration of the power he possessed.

I thought of Tipu Sultan, the eighteenth-century Indian mogul who was obsessed with the tiger and used its likeness as his constant emblem. Tipu Sultan's imperial banner had borne the words "The Tiger Is God." Looking up into Miguel's yellow eyes I felt the strange appropriateness of those words. The tiger was majestic and unknowable, a beast of such seeming invulnerability that it was possible to believe that he alone had called the world into being, and that a given life could end at his whim. The truth, of course, was far more literal. Miguel was a remnant member of a species never far from the brink of extinction, and his motivation for killing Ricardo Tovar probably did not extend beyond a behavioral quirk. He had a predator's indifference to tragedy; he had killed without culpability. It was a gruesome and unhappy incident, but as far as Miguel was concerned most of the people at the zoo had reached the same conclusion: he was just being a tiger.

Selling the Ranch

We had ridden up through Leyva Canyon, along the cottonwoods and seep willows bordering a dry creekbed, and now in the late afternoon we came to the top of a low mesa that overlooked the volcanic panoply of the Bofecillos Mountains. My horse, an amiable black gelding named Contento, stopped on his own authority and exhaled, the stale horse breath fluttering from his nostrils like heat exhaust. It sounded like a long, appreciative sigh.

The landscape before us appeared infinite and untouched—mesas, blunted peaks, broad thorny plains from which ramparts of raw lava rock rose and subsided like breaching whales. Vast as it was, it was only a small portion of Big Bend Ranch State Natural Area, the 300,000-acre chunk of Texas that had recently, after twenty years of negotiations, passed from private hands into the stewardship of the Texas Parks and Wildlife Department. The acquisition of Big Bend Ranch had, in one stroke, doubled the acreage of the state park system.

The new park was not open to the public yet, and would not be for at least another year. My visit here amounted to a kind of sneak preview, a sneak preview already 30 million years old. The Bofecillos Mountains, in the center of the park, were the remnants of a giant volcano that had exploded long ago, eventually leaving in its place a range of fractured and eroded landforms that were like the scattered stones marking the foundation of a vanished mansion. Like the rest of Big Bend Ranch, the Bofecillos had a desolate, haunted air. The country that Contento and I looked out upon seemed so ancient and elemental as to be immune to any further geological disturbances.

I looked east, searching the desert plains for some human mark, but could see only the endless clumpy growths of creosote and lechuguilla. There was no shade anywhere, just the evening shadows stretching outward from freestanding boulders.

"Where's the ranch house?" I asked John Guldemann.

"Got you lost, didn't I?" he laughed.

Guldemann dismounted and looped his horse's reins around an ocotillo stalk. Even allowing for his L. L. Bean sunglasses, he was every inch a working cowboy. He wore a black hat covered with dust and salt stains, chaps with old-fashioned leather fasteners, and jeans tucked into the tops of his boots. Guldemann was thirty-six, an El Paso native. He was an alumnus of Sul Ross State in

Alpine, where he had studied range-animal management and industrial arts. He had lived and worked on this ranch for the past ten years, during which time it was run by the Diamond A Cattle Company and was owned principally by Robert Anderson, the chairman of Atlantic Richfield. For the past three years Guldemann had been foreman, and when the state bought the ranch, he had been asked to stay on. He was now faced with making the mental leap from cowboy to park ranger.

We ambled along the summit of the mesa until we reached a deep smooth-sided gorge known as Cinco Tinajas. The place took its name from the five water holes that ages of flash floods had scoured out of the bedrock. Two or three of the *tinajas* were visible from where we stood, and beyond the bold vertical lines of the gorge we could see the broader declivity of Leyva Canyon, with its meandering strip of sand and luminous cottonwoods marking the route of the infrequent water.

"I've been here for ten years," Guldemann said, scanning the horizon, "and I still haven't been to every spot. It's hard for me to convey that to somebody, how big this place is. I can tell you about it and you can write it down, but I'm not sure you'll really get it. Before I moved to the ranch headquarters I lived at a camp called La Cienega. There's a place on this property where I can stand and look over to La Cienega, and it's fifteen miles away. And I can turn around, look the other way, and see the ranch headquarters, where I live now, and it's fifteen miles away. That's how big the ranch is."

Though Big Bend Ranch is only one third the size of its neighbor, Big Bend National Park, it is even more remote and isolated. On the average, the ranch sits at a higher elevation than the park. It is cooler and wetter, its fractured volcanic bedrock laced with groundwater. But like the national park, it is very much desert country. The ranch's springs and spindly waterfalls, its sudden flaring patches of green, are little more than grace notes. The real power of the region derives from its austerity. It is a compelling but welcoming place, an endless field of sculpted and compressed rock covered with a thin bloom of desert scrub.

On its southern border, the ranch extends all the way to the Rio Grande and incorporates much of the spectacular stretch of Ranch Road 170 that runs from Presidio to Lajitas. This is the most accessible part of the ranch, and the most beautiful, but it is still arid and ghostly. The water of the Rio Grande, as it threads itself through the rearing bulwarks of Colorado Canyon, is a dense, earth-toned flow, less like a river than some liquefied manifestation of the surrounding landscape. The Rio Grande supports a vibrant strip of greenery along its banks, but otherwise the water's life-giving influence is not immediately apparent. Twenty yards away from the edge of the river, there is nothing but vaulting rock leading upward to desert summits. The country's harshness is enthralling—at the same moment it lifts your heart and fills you with apprehension.

But now, as we stood on the mesa, with the light growing softer and softer, some of the land's fierceness began to melt away. We walked back to the horses, scattering chips of lava with our boots. On the way down we let the horses pick their way along the rocky ground of the mesa slope. The brush was thick here, and I was glad I was wearing chaps to deflect the stout spines of catclaw and ocotillo.

I had borrowed the chaps from the tack house at the ranch. They belonged to Bob Armstrong, the former commissioner of the General Land Office. Armstrong had first laid eyes on Big Bend Ranch in 1970, and then and there vowed to acquire it for the state. He had gone to the ranch for a weekend of hunting, driving all night through rain and snow. When day broke he beheld Big Bend Ranch draped uncharacteristically in white.

"I was totally unprepared to be that far south and see a snowscape in the Big Bend," Armstrong had told me. "As the snow melted and the scenery unfolded I thought it was the most remarkable place I'd seen in . . . well, in maybe ever."

Later, when Armstrong learned that Robert Anderson was willing to sell the property for $8 million, he borrowed the Senate photographer, hopped in the Land Office airplane, took a series of photographs of the ranch, and laid them out in the House and Senate lounges during the final days of the legislative session. Some officials were impressed; others were not (Governor Dolph Briscoe dismissed the ranch as "just scenery"). For various reasons—including political infighting, routine chicanery, and the stalwart objections of neighboring property owners who feared the purchase of the ranch at $36 an acre would raise their tax valuations—the money was not appropriated that session, or the next, or the next.

Over the years Anderson's offer remained more or less on the table. Armstrong left the Land Office in 1982, but he kept up his interest in the property. In 1988, the planets came into alignment: Armstrong by that time was a member of the Parks and Wildlife Department; Parks and Wildlife had a healthy acquisition budget; and the oil bust had made Texas a buyer's market. In the summer of 1988 the deal was made. There was a champagne closing in Marfa. For $8.5 million, less than the cost of refurbishing the Battleship *Texas,* less than it would cost a big city developer to build a downtown parking garage, Parks and Wildlife bought 469 square miles of primeval Texas.

Big Bend Ranch was scheduled to open to the public sometime in the next year or so. Exactly what sort of park it ultimately would be had not yet been decided by Parks and Wildlife, but its designation as a state natural area had already defined it as a place where development would be limited, where the land's inspiring and intimidating wildness would be largely preserved. The final form of Big Bend Ranch, however, was a touchy subject. Environmentalists were concerned that Parks and Wildlife was far too eager to open the park as soon as possible.

They felt that a treasure of such magnitude was worth a few extra years of sober appraisal in order to develop an unhurried master-use plan. There was debate on whether the Diamond A Company's remnant herd of Longhorn cattle should be allowed on the ranch, since they had a tendency to trample and despoil the springs. And neighboring ranchers—long devoted to the aggressive control of livestock predators—worried that the park would end up as a vast sanctuary for mountain lions and coyotes.

A white shepherd dog, aged and deaf, came hobbling up to greet us as we returned to the ranch headquarters. The dog's name was Grunt. He was thirteen years old. Guldemann explained that Grunt had been the ringbearer when he and his wife, Keri, were married on the ranch nine years ago. The ceremony had taken place at Rancho Viejo Springs, a watery oasis growing out of a parched igneous plain ten miles distant. John and Keri had taken their vows on horseback. Grunt, carrying the ring on a blue ribbon tied around his neck, had led the procession, and he had been followed by a preacher mounted on a dun mule that had the markings of a Jerusalem cross on its back.

We unsaddled the horses and I hung up Bob Armstrong's chaps in the tack house. The ranch head-quarters was made up of a cluster of buildings, the most prominent of them a white adobe house, its concrete porches buckled by massive cottonwood roots, which was built in the early part of the century by W. W. Bogel, an early owner of the ranch. The house was substantially added to by the Fowlkes brothers, Edwin and Manny, who came into this country a few years before World War II and spent the next two decades pulling together the acreage that became Big Bend Ranch.

We strolled up to the lodge, where Keri Guldemann was fluting the crust of a pecan pie. She was a slender, talkative woman, wearing jeans and a T-shirt featuring a cartoon map of Australia. The lodge, which was rustic in a prefab sort of way, had been built by a Houston oilman named Tufty McCormick, who owned the ranch after the Fowlkeses. He built it for friends who visited the ranch to hunt mule deer. Now the lodge served as a kind of bunkhouse for the Parks and Wildlife personnel—biologists, geologists, archaeologists, park planners, and bureaucrats—who came down in waves from Austin to oversee Big Bend Ranch's transition from a lordly cattle operation to a state park. Keri, like John, had been sworn into the service of the state when Parks and Wildlife bought the ranch. She was in charge of managing the lodge and cooking for the official visitors.

As it happened, I was the only guest that week. Keri checked to make sure that I was not a vegetarian—some of those Austin folks were—and then instructed John to make a mesquite fire outside for the ribeyes. We were joined for dinner by the Guldemanns' six-year-old son, Bucko, whose favorite horse I had been riding all afternoon.

"Thanks for the use of Contento," I said.

"Did you like him?" Bucko asked anxiously, as if everything depended on my approval of the horse.

They were, I thought, a classic ranch family in the midst of an unsettling transition. Their job was to redefine the purpose of the land on which they had been living for the past ten years, to preside over the dismantling of a working ranch and the creation of a subtly fashioned wilderness in its place. The acquisition of Big Bend Ranch represented, perhaps, the triumph in Texas of an urban ideal. The people who would be coming to the new state park, driving ten or twelve or fourteen hours from the cities where they lived, would be more than comfortable with the notion of land as unproductive and unyielding. They *wanted* it to be "just scenery." And there was a poignancy to the fact that while the Guldemanns were working hard to accommodate this new philosophy, they remained a living vestige of the old.

"As far as being a true cowboy," John Guldemann said wistfully, "the Diamond A was the place to be. It was all riding, all horses—it was a cowboy's dream."

There was still some ranch work to be done. Sixty head of Longhorns had come with the property, and the park plan called for them to stay, as a commemoration of Texas' ranching heritage. But the whole tenor of the place had inevitably changed. For instance, the historic isolation of the ranch had been invaded just this week by the installation of a satellite dish, whose random diet of images—from old Liberace movies to the Playboy Channel—had left Keri amused and alarmed. In the days of the Diamond A Cattle Company, Guldemann and his Mexican ranch hands used to round up hundreds of cattle and drive them on horseback from pasture to pasture, from one end of the ranch to the other. Now—as a Park Superintendent II—Guldemann spent far more time pushing paper than wrangling Longhorns.

For generations, back to the Fowlkes brothers and before, most of the Mexican ranch hands came from Mulato, a town just across the border that was settled by black Buffalo Soldiers who had deserted during the Indian wars. Most of the employees still lived in Mulato, but they were documented aliens now and employees of Parks and Wildlife. Their wages had doubled, and the timeless labor of ranch life had given way to forty-hour work weeks.

"They're better off now," Guldemann said, "but life is a lot different for them. For instance, they've all bought pickups, and at the end of the work week they'll drive home to Mulato. It used to be they'd work for twenty or twenty-five days, saddle up their horses, and ride across the river on trails that their fathers and grandfathers had used, trails that are centuries old. That'll never happen again. That's all over now."

I saw as much of the ranch as I could in the next few days, traveling with Guldemann in a four-wheel-drive pickup along dry washes and barely perceptible dirt roads overgrown with creosote. We passed desert bloom stalks top-heavy with perching hawks. Quail and roadrunners skittered out of the brush ahead of us, and mule deer, their coats as gray and parched as the caliche soil, bounded weightlessly up the mesa slopes.

As we lurched along, Guldemann never failed to point

out the network of rusting and patched pipelines that carried water to the distant reaches of the ranch. There were stock tanks and pumping stations as well, old dilapidated windmills, and stone corrals next to shearing decks with cement slabs. He stopped the truck on a hillside, and we got out to admire a pair of rusted machines that looked like giant meat grinders.

"These are shredder-chopper deals," he said. "During a drouth when there wasn't enough for the sheep to eat, the Fowlkes brothers would chop up sotol and feed it to them. In my opinion, this is the kind of thing you should put an interpretive plaque on.

"I want to see this ranch preserved in a lot of different ways. In Big Bend National Park there were a lot of things like this that they dismantled. There was a man there— I forget his name—who invented the ram pump. It worked on gravity feed. For every foot of drop you had ten feet of rise. The water would drop three feet, hit that ram pump, and shoot it up thirty feet. In Guadalupe Mountains National Park there was a pipeline that went up nearly vertical that was put in by a ranch manager and a few Mexican hands. It was an engineering *feat*. Out here—considering how harsh the land is and how little water there is—when you did something like that it was an accomplishment. They ought not to have torn those things down, but that's what they did. And not a clue that they were ever there."

Guldemann's passion for discarded equipment was infectious, and as we passed the hulks of ancient pickup trucks and the rusted-out piles of tin cans around old line camps and mining sites, I began to appreciate the continuum of human enterprise they recorded. Here was an old watering trough, circa 1935, no less profound a mark upon the landscape than the bedrock mortars in which the hunters and gatherers who lived here thousands of years ago ground up desert plants for food. Here was an abandoned adobe house, still with its vine trellis and rotting chairs, as mysterious in its way as the rock shelter where red-pigment renderings of snakes and deer and human handprints were so vague and faded that they looked like mineral deposits leaching out of the yellowish volcanic ash.

"This was an old wagon road," Guldemann pointed out as we drove to the top of Lower Guale Mesa. "See the hand-stacked rock on the side? It was probably built in the early nineteen hundreds. It went all the way to Presidio, which at that time was the closest supply point."

He stopped the truck where the road dropped precipitously downward through a craggy intrusion of lava rock. The old road was so steep here that we could see grooves in the bedrock, made when the wagons were lowered down the incline inch by inch, their brakes set and the horses hitched to the back. We walked down the unmaintained road for half a mile or so. Bloodroot grew through the cracks of the hand-laid abutments, and boulders and cobbles had reclaimed the roadbed.

"I don't know who built it," Guldemann admitted. "Like a lot of this ranch, there's no real history on it. There was a man named Guale Carrasco—this mesa is named for him—who ran cattle up in this country for a while. Did he build the road? A man named Leyva had a ranch up here too. Did he build it? I don't know."

We stood at the foot of the incline and looked out over Lower Guale Mesa. It spread out into the distance so far and so evenly that it appeared to be endowed with motion, like a slow, outgoing tide. Running like a thread across its immense surface was the track of the road, disappearing at the rim of the mesa and plunging into the river canyons below.

"Thinking about it now," Guldemann said, "it's an awful lot of trouble to go to town."

The place I most wanted to see at Big Bend Ranch was the Solitario. The Solitario is a laccolith, a circular formation five miles in diameter that was formed by a submerged fount of magma that raised the limestone bedrock like a blister and then collapsed, leaving behind a ragged basin. Seen from the air, the Solitario is a startling circular apparition, a series of concentric mountain ranges that make you think of a pond ripple sculpted in stone.

From the ground, its shape is not so apparent. I had imagined it as a kind of maze, its walls rearing up out of the desert, some dramatic geological secret at its heart. In truth the Solitario is so large I did not know I was in it until Guldemann pointed out the fact to me. The country was pretty much the same as it had been before, except that much of the visible rock was now limestone, its smoother contours now and again interrupted by a jagged volcanic vent plug rising from the ground like some gleaming fossil tooth.

But you could feel it. It felt like the Solitario—distant, secreted away, brutal in its isolation. We explored it for most of the morning, walking for miles through one of the narrow canyons—known as shutups—that drain the central basin. The shutup was a dry corridor, but the boulders that rose from its floor were polished and fluted by the passage of water. Along the sides of the canyon were massive blocks of limestone so disrupted long ago by the pressure of boiling magma that they looked like upended ocean liners about to sink stern first into the sea.

As we were driving out of the Solitario we spotted what looked like a cave high up on a hill. An old road led up to it, a faded series of switchbacks that had clearly not been driven in decades and that would be tricky even for Guldemann's Chevrolet Cheyenne. We left the truck at the bottom of the hill and climbed up. Near the top we found ourselves looking into the mouth of a half-dug mine. It went down into the rock for eight or ten feet, and then ended in a blunt dead end. In front of its mouth was a pile of broken and dislodged rock. Some nameless dreamer had doubtless staked everything long ago on the certitude that this hill was full of gold or silver or mercury, but in the end that pile of rock was all that his mine had yielded.

I wasn't moved to feel all that sorry for him, though. He had a fine view from here. He had the world to himself. He looked down upon a great curving horizon of desert, and beyond that to the gentle blue waves of distant mountains.

"Not a bad place to sit and contemplate," John Guldemann said, taking off his beat-up black hat. "You know, I kind of hate to give it up to Texas."

Swamp Thing

I was at an impressionable age when I saw my first snapping turtle. I was ten, standing on a low earthen dam in central Oklahoma and casting with a child-size Zebco into a gloomy lake not much bigger than a stock pond. The lake had a prehistoric feel to it. Dead trees rose from the water, the bare limbs swaying and creaking. The water itself was muddy and still. It looked as if it had been sitting there, immune to evaporation, since the beginning of time.

I had fouled my line on enough of those trees to begin feeling cranky and put-upon. And on the occasions when my plastic lure did reach the water—disappearing like a space probe into the toxic brown clouds of an inhospitable planet—it reported no signs of life. I was about to reel in the line when some unseen force gave a brutal tug that pulled my cork deep below the surface. The pressure from the bottom of the lake kept the fishing line as taut as a bowstring.

I was scared. This thing did not feel like a fish at all. I knew, as I cranked on the reel, that I had hooked something powerful and hostile, something that did not wish to be disturbed. The muscles in my arms were quivering with exhaustion by the time the creature finally appeared. I saw its head first, and then a neck so long I thought it was a snake, and finally the undersized shell, so small when compared with the thrashing mass of the body itself that it looked like a saddle on the back of a dragon.

Not knowing what else to do, I continued to reel in the line. The turtle was hooked in the mouth, and in its anger it kept flinging out its neck and snapping its jaws. It was the most ferocious, the most unworldly thing I had ever seen. The back of its head bristled with spiky warts, its shell was covered with algae and slime, and the skin of its front legs dragged the ground in loose, grotesque folds. As I hauled the turtle up the dam, it grasped the dirt with its sharp claws and contested every inch. But then, sensing a little slack in the line, it lunged forward with such force that its front legs cleared the ground. Paralyzed with awe, I stood and watched as it lumbered hissing toward me, its reptile eyes fixed on mine, its neck coiling and striking. I remember thinking, *It's coming to get me!*

My uncle, who was chopping firewood nearby, came trotting down the slope of the dam with an ax. Of course, I realized, this thing would have to be killed. It was an evil that must be vanquished. My uncle tried to cut off its head, but the turtle was quick and could retract its neck faster than the ax could fall. It died instead from a blow to the shell. After it stopped moving we scooped it up with the blade of the ax and tossed it back into the lake. Watching it sink, I began to cry. It was not pity I felt, but disgrace. That such a savage, primeval beast could be destroyed by a thoughtless child seemed to me a mistake, a cruel imbalance of nature. Until I encountered that snapping turtle, it had never occurred to me that the existence of another creature could be a greater wonder than my own.

I see them all the time now. When I'm strolling across the Congress Avenue bridge in Austin, I can often spot snapping turtles in the lake below as they paddle along the banks just beneath the surface. Snappers are immediately distinguishable from the other turtles that inhabit the lake—the red-ears, cooters, and stinkpots. For one thing, you never see snapping turtles basking on tree limbs or swimming companionably alongside your canoe. They prefer to linger in the dark ooze, now and then extending their necks like snorkels to take a breath from the surface. Their tails are thick, long, serrated, semi-prehensile. (Snappers in fast-moving water have been known to grasp a submerged branch with their tails to keep from being swept downstream.) Their bodies are squat, and the forward edges of their shells ride high above their necks like the collar of an ill-fitting coat. Except for the eerie parchment-yellow color of their eyes, they are dark all over.

In the early summer the females crawl out of the water to lay their eggs, their carapaces thick with drying mud.

Hiked up on their stubby legs, their necks extended, their long tails dragging in the dirt, they look more like dinosaurs than turtles. The females are on their way to build a nest somewhere nearby. They will dig a hole in the dirt and deposit twenty or thirty eggs, guiding each one into position with the hind feet like fussy hostesses arranging canapés on a tray. When all the eggs are laid, they will fill in the hole with dirt and then tamp it down by crawling back and forth. Their trip to the nest site and back will probably add up to less than half a mile, but for these awkward aquatic turtles it is an epic journey through an alien world.

Last summer, driving with my family to Houston, I saw one stalled with fright on the highway in the pine country just outside of Bastrop. I pulled the car over and we all got out to look at it. I told the kids to stand back, half afraid this low-lying reptile would leap up and grab one of them by the throat. But the turtle kept still, its neck tucked into its shell. It looked craven and terrified. A car roared by in the opposite lane and the turtle hugged the asphalt with its claws.

I wanted to get the turtle off the road, but that childhood encounter had made me a coward, and I was unwilling to reach down and touch it. I had read that the only safe way to pick up a snapping turtle is by the rear legs, or by the rear edge of the shell, "holding him well away from your body." An agitated snapper has an extensive biting range. It can fling its neck to the side like a whip and strike a target far back on its flank. This turtle was placid, but I didn't expect it to stay that way if I put my hands on it. It would, I thought, explode with rage. It would wriggle violently, release a gaseous cloud of musk, and lunge with its bony beak at my fingers.

I scooted the turtle forward with my foot, and it began

to crawl across the highway. Seeing no cars coming from either direction, I decided that the turtle would probably make it without my intervention, and gathered the family back into the car. Driving away, I watched in the rear-view mirror as it lumbered forward with excruciating slowness.

"Oh, no!" my wife called out as a car suddenly bore down upon the snapping turtle. The children cringed and hid their eyes. But the car passed harmlessly over the snapper, which continued on its journey, a dark slouching shape older than any human thought.

It surprised me how much we all had feared for the turtle in its moment of peril. Over the years, I had managed to conquer my atavistic revulsion to certain animals. It was nothing to me now to handle a snake or to brush with my finger the silken fur of a living bat, but a snapping turtle was still a kind of nightmare creature, and a part of me did not want to accept the idea that it was as vulnerable as the rest of creation. I knew that characterizing nature in this way was an ageless human fallacy, but I still could not quite get over the sensation that snapping turtles were the enemy. Their outward appearance was the manifestation of their grim consciousness. Snapping turtles lived, it seemed to me, in a constant state of wrathful agitation. They were like the souls of the damned—irredeemable, and loathsome even to themselves.

"A savage, cross-tempered brute." That's the way one biologist, in an otherwise unemotional volume on reptiles and amphibians, describes snapping turtles. "The general aspect," another authority queasily reports, "is so sinister that it imparts more of the feeling inspired by a thick-bodied, poisonous serpent than that of a turtle."

Snappers are ferocious, but it's important to remember that they are that way for a reason. They are not simply dyspeptic. Snapping turtles are underwater predators; they are attack vehicles. They lie in wait and strike at passing fish, or they paddle up to the surface and seize ducklings by the feet. Their strike has to be fast, the grip of their jaws tenacious.

Out of the water, a snapping turtle's small shell is an imperfect refuge, and so its best defense is to attack. "I have seen it snapping," a nineteenth-century naturalist wrote, "in the same fierce manner as it does when full-grown, at a time when it was still a pale, almost colorless embryo, wrapped up in its foetal envelopes, with a yolk larger than itself hanging from its sternum, three months before hatching."

Folklore says that when snappers bite they will not let go until it thunders. Not true, but they do like to hold on to their claim. They are also very efficient scavengers. This trait was supposedly once used by an Indian in northern Indiana, who exploited a snapping turtle, tethered to a long wire, to locate the bodies of drowning victims. And one of the worst practical jokes I ever heard of was perpetrated by a friend of mine when he was a rowdy adolescent. He put a baby snapping turtle into the purse of his friend's mother.

There are two kinds of snapping turtles, both of which are native to Texas. The common snapping turtle—*Chelydra serpentina*—is the smaller and more aggressive species. Its range extends throughout the entire eastern half of the continent, all the way from Canada (where it has been observed walking on the bottom of frozen streams beneath the ice) to Central America. It lives everywhere—lakes, rivers, swamps, even brackish tidal streams—but its prime habitat is sluggish, muddy water. Common snappers are not behemoths. The largest one ever caught in the wild weighed slightly less than seventy pounds, though one captive turtle that was kept in a swill barrel for two months ate its way up to eighty-six pounds.

Those figures are nothing compared with the mighty *Macroclemys temmincki,* the alligator snapping turtle. Alligator snappers can grow as large as sea turtles, up to 250 pounds or even more. Their heads are massive and blunt, their eyes lower on their heads than those of common snappers, their shells crowned with three high longitudinal ridges that look like miniature mountain ranges. Common snappers are common, but alligator snappers are increasingly rare. Alligator snapper meat has long been a steady seller in the fish markets of Louisiana, and the turtle population took a nose dive when Campbell's came out with a snapper soup in the early seventies. In Texas, alligator snappers are classified as a threatened species by the Parks and Wildlife Department. They tend to inhabit coastal drainages in East Texas, though they have made appearances as far west as Burleson County.

Unlike common snapping turtles, alligator snappers do not stalk their prey or seize it with serpentine strikes of their necks. They lie in wait, settled motionlessly in the cloudy water like boulders or stumps, their mouths hinged open to reveal a fluttering gob of tissue rooted to the lower jaw. When a fish spots the lure and enters the cavern of the turtle's mouth, it is either swallowed whole or neatly sliced. With this leisurely feeding strategy at their disposal, alligator snappers tend to have a less urgent temperament than their cousins. Though they look even more hideous than common snappers, they are comparatively docile.

Alligator snappers are strong and, in strange ways, agile. There is a report of a three-legged specimen climbing an eight-foot-high cyclone fence. The turtles have been known to shear off human fingers. All sorts of things—small alligators, entire beaver heads—have been found in their stomachs. For years it was a commonplace observation that an alligator snapping turtle was capable of biting a broom handle in two. Peter Pritchard, a Florida biologist who has written extensively on *Macroclemys temmincki,* decided to test this hypothesis. He waved a broom handle in front of a 165-pound alligator snapper to see if it really could bite it in half. It could.

"If common snapping turtles were as big as alligator snapping turtles," an East Texas herpetologist named William W. Lamar told me, "they would take bathers regularly."

Several years ago, when Lamar was the curator of herpetology at the Caldwell Zoo in Tyler, I dropped in to see his alligator snapper collection. The zoo had three specimens, including a baby that was kept in an aquarium tank in the reptile house. The first time I saw it I wasn't sure it was even a living thing. It was settled down at the bottom of the tank, eerily still, its jaws hinged open as if in some epic yawn and its right foreleg raised like a pointer's. The only things moving were the lure inside its mouth and a doomed fish that swam near the surface. Lamar remarked that the snapper looked like a log with a worm on it.

We left the baby still angling for the fish and went outside to look at the larger specimens. Another curator climbed over a fence and waded into a pond. He looked around on the bottom a bit, then reached down with both hands and hauled up a forty-five-pound turtle, lifting it by either end of the shell. The alligator snapper's name was Eugenia. She was dark and mucky and immense, a ghastly apparition from the dawn of time.

Lamar looked down at this strange beast admiringly. Eugenia seemed to me not a animal but an entity—a moving, moss-covered rock. I asked Lamar if alligator snappers were intelligent. What I wondered was: Do they think?

"If one looks at intelligence as the ability to learn functions that are nontraditional," he said, "I don't know. Nobody's ever trained one of these things to dance. A common snapper is lacking in personality to me. They do what they do with a lot of aggressive verve, but they're boring. They're like somebody you'd expect to meet in a casino in Vegas. But my opinion of alligator snappers is they're a lot more receptive to stimuli than most people think. A lot more goes on in their lives than most people imagine."

Some months later I acquired a snapping turtle. It was a baby, a common snapper, hatched from a clutch of eggs that a reptile fancier had discovered on the banks of the San Marcos River. A mutual friend delivered the turtle to me one day in a bucket.

I went to the pet shop and bought a twenty-gallon aquarium, a filter, and a pile of decorative rocks. When the aquarium was all set up and running, I put on a pair of gloves and picked the turtle up from behind. To my surprise, it didn't thrash about and try to bite my hand. It merely kept its head retracted into its shell as far as it would go.

The turtle was only a few inches long, no more than

several months old. When I put it in the water, it sank to the bottom like a piece of lead and then began to scramble frantically upward without success. It didn't seem to be able to swim. I reached into the water and set it on one of the rocks, and it craned its neck up, up, up until its nostrils were above the surface. And there the turtle stayed.

"Let's call him Sam," my oldest daughter said, and that became his name, though we never used it. He was always just "the snapping turtle." He would lie there on the rock all day and all night, blinking, breathing. I dropped little pellets of turtle food on top of the water, but the turtle would not eat with me in the room. After I left, the food disappeared.

The little aquarium filter chugged along diligently, and I changed the water once a day, but the moment I put the turtle into the clean water it immediately turned into a fetid bog. I was tired of the maintenance, but I grew oddly fond of the snapping turtle. I found him more interesting than odious. His silent, patient, undemanding presence was somehow restful to me.

Nevertheless, after a few months I had had enough. The whole house was beginning to stink. I decided to take the turtle and release him back into the San Marcos.

The night before I let him go, however, I dropped a few pellets of turtle food into the tank and hid behind the door, watching. I saw the turtle track the food with his eyes as it sank slowly down to him. When a pellet was several inches away he shot his neck out with a startling and unnecessary motion, snapped his dinner savagely in half, then gulped it down with urgent, gagging movements of his throat.

The kids and I took him down to a murky little eddy

cut into a bank of the river. I put on my gloves, set him into the water, and he was gone in an instant in a swirl of mud. I suddenly felt an unexpected pang, of what I cannot imagine.

We walked along the bank looking for him. We wanted to say good-bye to this creature that had never had any need or cognizance of us—that just was. I wondered if he would survive. If he did, if he was not eaten by another snapping turtle, if he was not caught on a boy's fishing line, he might live ten or twenty years, spending the winters denned up under cutbanks, the summers loitering in the mud. He would grow up to replace the turtle whose death I had caused so many years ago, and whose savage, unappeasable spirit was still alive, still snapping at me in my dreams.

The Roof of Eden

It was evening, the long summer twilight of the Front Range. I sat on the veranda of the Stanley Hotel in Estes Park, Colorado, drinking peppermint tea from a crystal cup while violet-green swallows coasted above the lawn in perfect arcs of flight. The air was cool. I rubbed my hands on the warm teacup and wished I had bought that sweatshirt after all, the one with the words "Rocky Mountain National Park—75th Anniversary" silk-screened below a noble profile of a bighorn sheep.

Seventy-five years. Idly, I did the math—27,393 mountain evenings such as this one. Several hundred evanescent generations of birds and chipmunks and tundra flowers winking in and out of existence upon the Rockies' eternal facade. Measured against the peaks above me, which gleamed like steel in the flaring sunlight, seventy-five years was so small a unit of time as to seem theoretical.

And no doubt in another few nanoseconds of mountain time the sprawling tourist village of Estes Park—with its water slides and taffy shops, its souvenir boutiques selling hand-blown glassware, porcelain gnomes, and full-color busts of John Wayne—would prove to be as transient as alpenglow.

"A concentration of beautiful lateral valleys, intersected by meandering watercourses, ridged by lofty ledges of precipitous rock, and hemmed in upon the west by vast piles of mountains climbing beyond clouds. . . ."

That was how Rufus B. Sage, probably the first man to write about the area, described its appeal in 1843. Sage was traveling by himself—he was, he wrote, "one of the world-hating *literati,*" a man with a craving for cosmic loneliness. It is hard to imagine a better place for him than these immense glacial valleys and knife's-edge summits with their plumes of drifting snow. But the mountains were not entirely uninhabited. The high country still bore traces of rock walls along which Indians had stampeded game. In Sage's time, Utes and Arapahos still raided each other's encampments at the base of the mountains, and enterprising braves would climb alone to the highest peaks, where they would lie in wait beneath piles of brush and grab eagles by the feet. But by and large it must have thrilled Rufus Sage to see how thoroughly the human presence was muffled in a blanket of solitude.

Today, Rocky Mountain is one of the most-visited national parks in the country. About 2.5 million people come here every year, most of them passing through the gateway town of Estes Park and proceeding across the national park along the alpine highway known as Trail Ridge Road. The majority of tourists never leave their cars—they just drive on across the Continental Divide, admiring the scenery, on their way to somewhere else. But in summer the trails still teem with world-hating literati, most of them content with even a vestige of "the far-spreading domains of silence and loneliness" that Rufus Sage discovered.

By the time I finished my second cup of tea, streetlights were coming on in the dark hollow of Estes Park, though the peaks above were still spotlighted by the setting sun. I walked through the lobby of the old hotel, stopping to scrutinize the portrait of its namesake that hung near the billiard room. "F. O. Stanley," read the plaque, "Inventor—Industrialist—Lover of Mankind."

Stanley, along with his twin brother, was the inventor of the Stanley Steamer, a sprightly motor car that once hit a speed of 127 mph. One of the cars still stands in the hotel lobby as a curiosity—an elegant contraption with a mahogany steering wheel, lantern headlights, and a winding horn mounted on the side of the car.

Stanley used to pick his guests up at the train station in Loveland—guests such as Enrico Caruso, John Philip Sousa, and Theodore Roosevelt—and transport them sixteen miles via Stanley Steamer to his marvelous hotel. He was an abstemious sort and only grudgingly set aside one room in which his guests could smoke, a room he himself never entered. As a lover of mankind, he was selective. He would sit out on the porch and turn away guests whose looks he did not find promising.

He died on the porch in 1940, and over the years his hotel went to seed in an elegant and creepy way. (Stephen

King spent several nights in Room 237, working on *The Shining*.) Though it has recently been restored, its grand old mustiness has not been tampered with. My room was like an attic bedroom in my grandmother's house—with old-fashioned, two-button light switches, a lumpy four-poster bed, and a constant mountain breeze through the open window.

The next morning I got up early and drove through town on my way to the park. The main street of Estes Park was already crowded with lumbering RV's and mountain bikes. The traffic police wore shorts and baseball caps, and instead of guns they had water bottles strapped to their belts. On the rock facade of a liquor store a climber was practicing his holds, shifting his weight fluidly from limb to limb with slow, spidery motions.

I paid my entrance fee and drove up to Bear Lake. The parking lot was huge, and almost full. Four nuns piled out of the car ahead of me and, with their habits blowing in the breeze, began to lace up their hiking boots. I ambled along the nature trail around Bear Lake. The lake was a quiet expanse of dark, tannic water, its surface protected by the fringing firs and pines. In its waters the sharp, bare peaks above were reflected with eerie fidelity. Longs Peak was the highest—14,255 feet, almost a mile higher than where I stood. From this angle, the peak did not have the soaring splendor of an isolated summit. It was simply the highest in a series of distant waves of gray rock.

But it had always been a commanding goal. A trip to the summit and back, I had been told, takes twelve hours, and for much of the way it is a taxing scramble across boulder fields and narrow mountain defiles with woozy downward vistas.

"It is one of the noblest of mountains," wrote Isabella Bird, who climbed Longs Peak in 1873, "but in one's imagination it grows to be much more than a mountain. It becomes invested with a personality. . . . Thunder becomes its voice, and the lightnings do it homage."

Bird was forty years old when she climbed Longs Peak—"a quiet, intelligent-looking, dumpy English spinster." Her health was not good. She suffered from a chronic spinal condition that she sought to relieve by constant travel. Though she spent only three months in the Rockies, she wrote a classic account (*A Lady's Life in the Rocky Mountains*) of her adventures. Her prose, like her nature, was excitable. She made the ascent of Longs Peak in the company of Rocky Mountain Jim, a rough-but-courtly sort, whose face had been mutilated in a grizzly bear attack, leaving him with only one eye. His ruined face and "dark, lost, self-ruined life" intrigued her. "Desperado," she reported, "was written in large letters all over him."

Her account of the assault on the peak is a masterpiece of throbbing Victorian prose. "Jim dragged me up," the fatigued adventuress wrote, "like a bale of goods, by sheer force of muscle." During the trip, he hauled her with his lariat, severed her entangled frock with his knife, and delivered her to the summit, where they were "up-lifted above love and hate and storms of passion, calm amidst the eternal silences."

Rocky Mountain Jim apparently fell gloomily in love with Isabella during the ascent, but when they came back to earth she did not encourage him. "He is a man whom any woman might love," she wrote her sister, "but no sane woman would marry." Bird left the Rockies and went on to more adventures in the Far East. The next year Jim was shot in a dispute, probably over a woman. He died, but for a while it looked as if he might recover. "It is hard to die," a friend remarked, "in the wonderful air of that great altitude."

I wandered for an hour or so along the trails leading from Bear Lake. A browsing deer looked up at me, folded its ears forward, and snorted as if it had a cold. A weasel rippled across the trail, half concealed itself beneath a boulder, and watched my progress with curious intensity. On the way back to the parking lot I passed through a grove of young aspens, their green, paddle-shaped leaves riffling in the wind and casting a lattice of shadow on the forest floor.

This was the low country, the montane woodlands dominated by ponderosa pine. When I got into my car and drove up Trail Ridge Road, I quickly passed through the sub-alpine zone, with its forests of fir and Engelmann spruce, and then past the contorted, wind-stripped trees at timberline to the tundra itself, the vast, sloping, high-mountain carpet with its cushion plants and lichens and pinpricks of yellow flowers.

I stopped the car at an overlook and got out, breathing in the austere air and looking down at a sea of meadows and conifer forests. Feeling light-headed and eager to learn, I joined a tundra walk departing from the Alpine Visitor Center. The ranger was young, with a scholarly air and a neat beard. The brim of his campaign hat sat so squarely above his brow it looked as if it had been adjusted with a carpenter's level. He pointed out alpine avens, skypilot, and the stunted willows eaten by the ptarmigans that winter in the tundra. To illustrate his lecture, he pulled a stuffed marmot out of a plastic bag. The marmot was a shapeless lump of fur, as stiff as cardboard.

"In the winter, while he's hibernating," the ranger said, "you could pick this guy out of his burrow, play a game of football with him, and come summer he'd have no recollection. All he does during the summer is lounge around and pig out till he gets fat, and in the winter he sleeps it off. If Shirley MacLaine is right, I'm coming back as a marmot."

On the way back down Trail Ridge I stopped to observe several living marmots that were lying on the tundra rocks and now and then opening their mouths and chirping like birds. The marmots were obese, and their scrappy fur was as full of dings as a bad carpet, but they were not the comical rodents I had expected. They had a certain air, a nobility of repose that made me think of the stone lions outside the New York Public Library.

That night I set up a tent in the campground in Moraine Park as two black squirrels with long, tufted ears looked on inquiringly. Moraine Park, a commodious meadowland banked by glacial ridges, was scoured out of the bedrock by a creeping tongue of ice. The glacier has been gone for 13,000 years, but its mighty work is still thrillingly apparent. The marshlands were dewy. The meandering stream was a garish silver band, and the whole expanse looked glimmering and fresh, as if it had just hours before been hatched from beneath the ice.

There was a slide show that night in the Moraine Park amphitheater, and I followed the other campers as they ambled along the road in the dark. Through the bright windows of the RV's I could catch glimpses of people playing cards, watching TV, or reading paperbacks with florid, die-cut covers. At the amphitheater the ranger stood at a lectern made of rock, a microphone clipped to his tie. Behind him was a projection screen, and beyond that the moraine and the distant tundra slopes. The moonlit peaks looked as rumpled and comfortable as corduroy.

The ranger showed slides of ponderosa pine and bitter-brush, of elk-scarred aspen and broad-tailed hummingbirds. The campfire near his feet burned itself out quickly, and as the program wore on, the darkness increased so that the mountain peaks showed only as a dark, jagged line across the star field. The air was so still and silent that each *ka-chunk* sound the projector made as it advanced a slide seemed to echo with a satisfying heft.

"Someone once said," the ranger concluded in a low and reverent voice, "that next to freedom, national parks were the greatest idea America ever had."

The next morning I was up early to mull that one over. It was first light, and fog pooled in the hollows and distant canyons. Each of these canyons, each tiny fissure branching off from the glacial valley, turned out, when seen through my binoculars, to be a broad avenue leading to the still-unseen heart of the American wilderness. I cherished the notion that I was free to follow any of these gorges, for as far as I wanted to go—to disappear, if I chose, into those foggy valleys.

In 1917, two years after Rocky Mountain National Park officially opened, a college student named Agnes Lowe did just that. The *Denver Post* announced her intention of dashing into the "Garden of Eden" clad only in a toga of animal skins. This was a publicity stunt. Young ladies did not enter the wilderness alone and unequipped in 1917, and two thousand people assembled to watch "the modern Eve" romp off into the mountains.

The next day a man in a robe, billing himself as "the new Adam," announced his intention to follow Miss

Lowe into the Garden. He appears to have been crazy, and did not get far before being dissuaded by park personnel. Meanwhile Eve had a few rough days— "Nearly froze last night," she wrote in charcoal on the bark of a tree—but soon adjusted. When a group of hikers encountered her, they saw that she had shed her cave-woman costume and was roaming through the sunshine "à la Nature."

Miss Lowe allotted only a week to her role as Eve, and soon returned to college. But as I walked through the marshy grass in Moraine Park and trained my binoculars upward—up through the dense conifers to the tundra and finally to the crags and spires of naked rock—I imagined she was here still, an ageless alpine nymph giddy with the license of the wilderness.

"I believe there is a God!" poor Rocky Mountain Jim had blurted out to Isabella Bird during their ascent of Longs Peak, as the day dawned beatifically below them. It was an understandable outburst. The park is one of those places whose beauty can affect you like a seizure. Is it any wonder that Jim found himself overpowered with belief, doomed as he was, as he stood there with his beloved upon the roof of Eden?

The Man Nobody Knows

At seven o'clock in the morning, the valley of the Inn River was still dark. It would take another hour or so for the winter light to begin leaking over the crests of the mountains. Though the sun had not yet risen, the temperature was mild, and the streets of Innsbruck were half submerged in a slurry of melted snow. High, high above the city, along the ramparts of the Alps, the lights of villages and lodges shone like distant stars.

I had come to Innsbruck to learn about the Stone Age man whose mummified body had recently been found in a nearby glacier, and when I glanced up at those peaks I tried to look at them through a Neolithic lens. A traveler walking through this valley five thousand years ago, I imagined, might also have seen clusters of illumination beckoning from villages far away in those mountain meadows. There would have been fewer lights, of course, and they would have flickered rather than held steady, but perhaps they would have filled the hiker's mind with the same sort of awe and isolation I felt today gazing up at the Alps. Measured against those mountains—which looked even deeper and more eternal than the black sky behind them—five thousand years ago seemed very near at hand.

Indeed, it was hard not to think of the man in the glacier as being, in some weird sense, still alive. One of the names the press had given him—besides *Der Eismann, Der Gletschermann, Der Tirolmann,* and *Der Similaunmann*—was *Otze.* This name, derived from the Otztaler Alpen region where the body had been found, had a mocking, mascotlike ring to it, as if the man were not in on the joke of his own long-ago death. In photographs he appeared hideously deceased but also somehow aware. With his dried-out eyeballs staring blankly out of their sockets, he seemed more than a relic from the past—he seemed like an emissary.

Though the Iceman's body was shriveled, gnawed upon, hairless, and as tough as rawhide, it was otherwise remarkably intact, and its discovery had intrigued scientists and casual newspaper readers around the world. Lying for five thousand years or more in the glacial ice, the body and its effects constituted an almost miraculous time capsule from the waning centuries of the Late European Stone Age, an era more precisely known as the Late Neolithic Age.

The people who lived in central Europe then were farmers and animal herders, hunters and artisans. They tended their crops of wheat or barley and lived in wooden houses with plank floors, with corrals for their livestock nearby. Some of their villages were walled and fortified, some were raised on pilings at the edges of marshy lakes. With implements made from deer antler, they quarried flint for the manufacture of the stone axheads and daggers that would soon be rendered obsolete by the metallurgical revolution that ushered in the Bronze Age.

Late Neolithic Europeans buried their dead in communal tombs made of massive stone blocks. Within these megalithic vaults the dead lay in rows, bundled up like sleeping children, the males lying on their right side, the females on their left. Near them were arranged various tools and treasures for use in the next world—axes, knives, beads of limestone and shell.

Finds of such artifacts are not uncommon. Over the years archaeologists have unearthed many of these burials, with their rows of broken skeletons and formal grave goods. But the Iceman is unique. He died alone, apparently by accident, and lay undiscovered beneath a thick shield of ice as the megalithic tombs crumbled and the world he had known passed away. The things that were found with him were not ceremonial objects but the tools and weapons and personal effects of everyday use. And his body was preserved as a mummy, though not a stately, embalmed mummy like the kind left behind by the Egyptian Pharaohs of the Old Kingdom, entombed in their pyramids during the same epoch that the Iceman was sealed in his glacier. His body had not been preserved by elaborate funerary rituals, but by atmospheric chance, and, when it was found, it was whole.

The Iceman's leathery hide still bore its ancient tattoos, and within his body's desiccated organs there was a potential diagnostic treasure trove of enzymes, food remnants, parasites, and genetic material that might one day be able to shed light on the Iceman's health at the time of his lonely death.

For the time being, he resided in a freezer vault at the University of Innsbruck's School of Anatomy. "No, no," I was told by Werner Platzer, chairman of the anatomy department, when I asked to see him. "It is unpossible!"

Allowing anyone in to see the mummy, he explained, could provoke an international incident. The Iceman's ownership would ultimately be decided in favor of Italy—though the body would remain in Innsbruck three years while scientists completed their testing—but when I visited, it was a matter of dispute between that country and neighboring Austria. The body had been found fifty to sixty miles south of Innsbruck, on a high mountain pass near the main crest of the Alps. This crest is an important watershed—moisture from its southern slopes drains into the Adriatic Sea, while rain and snowmelt on its northern side feed the rivers and streams of the Austrian Tirol. At the end of World War I, the Treaty of Versailles stipulated that this watershed was the border between Italy and Austria. Later on, the border was fixed by a series of stone markers.

These markers did not, however, follow the exact contours of the watershed; hence the custody battle. The Iceman was found about a hundred yards within the Austrian side of the watershed. If the watershed was the border, he was clearly Austrian. If, however, the true border was represented by the stone markers, then the Iceman belonged to the Italians, since a line drawn between the two nearest markers placed him in the Italian state of South Tirol.

Until the exact ownership of the Iceman was determined, he remained off-limits to the public and the press, and so I had to content myself with looking through a stack of photographs in the university's Institute for Pre- and Proto-History. The office door was decorated with cartoons from Austrian newspapers and magazines whose German gag lines I could not read, but which showed the mummy's wrinkled body propped up in a railway carriage for his trip into the twentieth century, or being pulled apart in a tug-of-war across the Italian-Austrian border.

The first photograph of the body showed it lying face down in a pool of slush, just beginning to emerge from the ice that had contained it for millennia. The back of the Iceman's head was as smooth and round and weathered as some archaic pottery vessel, and beneath it were his wizened shoulders, the scapular bones protruding like a pair of folded wings. Another picture showed him whole, after his removal from the ice, lying on a steel dissecting table at the university. His left arm was flung awkwardly across his chest, rigid as a stick. The skin was stretched taut over his skeleton. Something had long ago chewed away his genitals, but a wad of plant fiber—the lining of what had once been a shoe—still covered his right foot.

I studied the close-ups of the Iceman's ghastly face. Hairless and shriveled, with the tip of the nose and upper lip missing, it still bore the stamp of a particular identity. There was a gap between his front teeth, exposed now by the absence of the lip; in life it would have showed whenever he smiled. His chin was sharp, his eyes were open. The tissue of one eye was white, the other piebald. A blurry blue cross was tattooed on the back of his knee, and there were more tattoos on the small of his back, three discreet columns of horizontal lines.

The Iceman had been found at an altitude of 10,500 feet on September 19, 1991, by a German couple on their way home from climbing Finail Peak in the Tirolean Alps. They spotted the body near a high mountain pass known as the Hauslabjoch, in a field of receding ice that had once been a nameless tributary to the Similaun Glacier. Not far from the Hauslabjoch is another pass, the Niederjoch, which is lower by some 600 feet. For centuries shepherds from the villages to the south led their sheep over the Niederjoch and down into the long valley, the *ferner,* beyond it. Sometimes, when the Niederjoch was covered with snow, the shepherds would detour to the west and take the Hauslabjoch.

Perhaps that is the detour the Iceman took so long ago. It was no accident that he lay in the path of modern climbers and hikers. The mountain terrain dictated, then as now, where people would walk.

Between his time and ours, however, the tongues of the glaciers had crept up and down these steep mountain defiles, advancing and receding with the rhythm of a tide. When the Iceman tried to climb over the Hauslabjoch, the glaciers were in retreat. The ground he lay on as he was dying probably was clear of ice, but over time the glacier came back and covered it, burying him until he was revealed during the warm autumn of 1991.

Rainer Henn, director of the Institute of Forensic Medicine at the University of Innsbruck, had already examined a half-dozen bodies that had come out of the thawing glaciers that year, including the remains of two climbers lost in 1934. When he entered his office on

September 23, there was a note on his desk alerting him to the discovery of yet another victim of the mountains.

By law, Henn is required to remove any such body from the ice, perform an autopsy on it, and determine the cause of death. When he took a helicopter up to the Similaun Glacier, he had no idea that the corpse he was about to inspect was a Stone Age relic.

For four days, ever since the German couple had discovered the Iceman and notified the warden of a nearby mountaineering hut, hikers and climbers had dropped in on the site; some of them had gathered up pieces of equipment or clothing that were lying near the body. Reinhold Messner, the legendary mountain climber, had happened by as well, and had been struck by the apparent antiquity of the body and the strange blue marks on its back. He thought it might be four hundred years old.

"When I came to this place," Henn told me, "the body was still partly covered with ice. I only saw the back of the head and part of the back. I had not the faintest idea how important it was. I only knew that this body must have been completely mummified before it was covered with snow."

Henn and his colleagues began hacking away with mountaineering axes at the ice enclosing the body, and dug a small trench to channel away the slush water that had accumulated in the warm sunlight. In the trench, Henn found a small stone dagger with a long wooden handle.

"When I saw this knife," he said, "I had the idea that this man was very old—I had no idea *how* old—and from this moment I ordered all these people to be most careful while getting the body out of the ice."

The body was wrapped in plastic and taken by helicopter and ambulance to the University of Innsbruck, where it was examined the next morning by Konrad Spindler, the dean of the Institute for Pre- and Proto-History. By now, most of the Iceman's equipment and the remains of his clothing had been recovered as well. There were a few strips of plaited grass, which might have been a shoulder cape or a sleeping mat, and pieces of an animal-hide jacket, finely stitched with threads of twisted grass. There was part of a bow and a leather quiver filled with fourteen arrows, two of which were notched and feathered and the others presumably unfinished. Another leather case, containing a flint scraper, a ball of resin, and a few flint tips, was thought to be a repair kit for the arrows. Then there was the small flint knife that Henn had found and a simple stone amulet, as well as several broken pieces of wood that, when fitted together, suggested a pack frame.

There was also an ax, in superb condition, with a long wooden handle to which a precision blade was still attached with rawhide lashes and some sort of ancient putty. After studying the ax, Spindler had first decreed that the frozen corpse dated from the early Bronze Age, about two thousand years before the birth of Christ, but this estimate turned out to be off by a millennium. The ax blade, with its duck beak shape and low hammered edges, fit the profile of a blade from the early Bronze Age, but it was not bronze, the alloy of copper and tin that transformed the Neolithic world. The Iceman's blade was almost pure copper, probably quarried from a mountainside and pounded into shape rather than smelted and cast—the product of an earlier technology. In addition, carbon 14 tests on the Iceman's body and on the plant fiber lining his remaining shoe confirmed that he had lived between 4,800 and 5,500 years ago.

As a relic, the man could be classified and dated. But it was the sense of something that could never be known—the mystery of his human identity—that moved me when I looked at those photographs. It was odd how a five-thousand-year chasm of time created as much a sense of intimacy as of distance. I found it impossible to think of the Iceman for long without feeling sorry for him, thinking about his solitary death and imagining the apprehension, the dread of the family he never came home to.

Sitting in Konrad Spindler's office, I asked him what he had felt when he had first seen the body. A meticulous man in a blue suit and steel-rimmed glasses, Spindler studied the pink message slips lined up in ranks on his immaculate desk.

"At first I did not feel any emotion," he said. "There was too much work to be done." A faint smile played across Spindler's impassive face. "But perhaps later," he said, "I thought of Mr. [Howard] Carter, when he opened the tomb of Tutankhamen."

We talked about who the man might have been and what he might have been doing that autumn on the Hauslabjoch. "Perhaps he was a shepherd with goats," Spindler mused, and immediately I wondered whether the Iceman had a dog to help him with the herd, and whether the dog had died with him or found his way back home.

"There are copper mines in these valleys," Spindler went on. "We have here natural outcroppings of copper. Perhaps he was looking for nuggets. Surely in the winter he must have lived in a settlement in the valley—but we don't know whether north or south. Surely he had contacts with others. The tattoos couldn't be made by himself. They had to be made by another person.

"His bow is unfinished. Perhaps the original bow of this man was stolen or broken, and he went down to the valley and fetched wood for the new bow. Perhaps in the evening as he sat by the fire he worked on the bow.

"His clothes are made from hide, from deer. Very fine and exactly made." Spindler pointed to the stitching on his own suit. "The stitches are very fine. But there are some other stitches that are very raw. So we think maybe this man tore his clothes and repaired them himself, but very raw."

I asked Spindler if he had a guess about what happened to the man.

"I think he died by coldness," he said. "He lost his way, and he died by coldness. In this time—late September—you have degrees under zero Fahrenheit. If you lose your way in a blizzard, you don't have any chance to go on living."

Whatever terrible misfortune befell the Iceman in life, he became, as it was later explained to me, "a very lucky corpse." It is widely believed that the bodies of people who are lost in the deep freeze of a glacial landscape remain as preserved and undefiled as Snow White in her glass casket. In reality, they are transformed in fascinating and gruesome ways—their limbs are sheared off by the movement of the glacier, their fatty tissues turn as pale and hard as plaster. The body of the Iceman underwent its own metamorphosis, but through a series of remarkable occurrences it was in far better shape after five thousand years in the ice than most bodies after a few months.

"You would perhaps like to see some of our other glacier bodies?" one of Professor Henn's assistants inquired when I dropped in at the university's Institute for Forensic Medicine. He led me down the hall and unlocked the door to a small museum of forensic science. It was a strange place. There were rows of jars filled with people's heads floating in greenish preservative fluid, their eyes and mouths gaping open. There was an exhibit of the ropes, dog leashes, chains, and other constrictive devices that had been removed from hanging victims, and in glass cases nearby there were several of the victims themselves, or at least what was left of them after several weeks of hanging from a tree limb in the forest.

"Here is how a glacier body looks normally," my guide said, indicating a human form lying full length in a display case. "This one fell into the glacier in 1923. He came out in 1952." The man under the glass was still tangled in his mountaineering ropes, still wearing his boots, crampons, and sweater, but he was broken and disjointed and his head was so shriveled and papery it reminded me of an onion. Inside the ice, subject to cold, humidity, and lack of oxygen, the parts of the body that had once stored fat—the adipose tissues—had turned hard and pale. The organs had long ago rotted away, so all that was left were bones, teeth, fingernails, and this crust of adipose flesh.

Henn joined us and took me to an examining room to show me the body of another climber. "This person came from Vienna," he said, looking down at the torso of a man. "He disappeared in 1934. We found him three or four weeks before we found the Iceman."

The body had most likely lost its lower half when the glacier moved above it, grinding it against the rocks. One of the man's arms was mummified, the hand pinched into a claw and the nails weathered and blackened. But the rest of the body was like a badly chipped plaster statue.

Henn told me that when the man had been found, he still had his railway tickets and a membership card to a mountaineering club in his pocket. The climber had been in his robust sixties when he died. Even now his glasses rested on what was left of the bridge of his nose, and a dental plate lay casually on his chest. His face had turned into a shell of stony tissue, but a scrap of beard was still attached to his chin like a piece of coarse sandpaper.

"This is what we usually see," Henn explained, looking down at the body, which looked less like human remains than an oddly shaped piece of soft, crumbly rock. "It was a chain of lucky circumstances that preserved the Iceman in such an outstanding way."

Those circumstances began with the site of his death. The place where the Iceman was found was a flat shelf of rock about two hundred feet wide, with a narrow cavity running through it. This stone trench was ten or fifteen feet deep, a logical place to take shelter in the face of a sudden storm. Presumably this is what the man did, though he died anyway, and afterward foxes or perhaps vultures began to feast on the body. But for some reason they stopped. Maybe another storm came, covering the body with snow and driving the scavengers to lower elevations.

Had it lain there under the snow for long, the Iceman's body would have been transformed, as were the bodies of the climbers in the forensic museum; but something else happened instead. Most likely the dry autumn winds of the Alps—the *foehn*—blew away the first protective covering of snow, exposing the body and leaching it of moisture. Within several weeks it became a mummy—a shrunken, dehydrated, but otherwise perfect husk of the man who had once inhabited it.

The rock trench in which the body lay became a crypt. Over time the ice that had once covered the spot came back, but inside his narrow crevice the Iceman was spared the crushing weight of the glacier. And because this terrain on the Hauslabjoch pass was flat, the glacier barely moved, so there was no damage from the pulverizing scree that a glacier carries with it when it slowly glides downslope.

Protected from all the elements that would normally have destroyed it—bacteria, scavengers, chemical transformation, the shifting and sliding of the landscape itself—the Iceman's body lay undisturbed in its frozen chamber. When it emerged, it was in good enough shape for Henn to plan an autopsy to determine whether the man died from hypothermia, as Spindler suspected, or from some other cause.

"Legally," Henn told me, "I have to do an autopsy to find out how he died. It will be difficult and take a long time. First, we will find out by computer thermography what is inside. Because the body is so hard, we will have to use not a scalpel but an electric saw. We will make small incisions at the sides so we do not damage his shape."

But the autopsy would be months in the future. In the meantime, teams of scientists from all over the world had begun to analyze the Iceman's equipment, his clothes, even the pollen found frozen in the ice near his body.

"We are looking for all that could be of interest," Platzer told me later that afternoon in his office in the anatomy building. "For instance, parasites—ecto- or indo- parasites. We are looking at what is inside the stomach. And we are looking at the skin, to see if he has the same cells in his skin as we have in ours. It is a very interesting question: Had the man lived outside and was therefore very sunny brown? Had he such cells as are necessary for the sunny brown of the skin? Will we find any antigens? If this man has the same antigens as we do, then the same ills are in his way of life."

I asked once again if I could see the body, but Platzer denied my request with a polite wave of his pipe. He did consent, however, to show me the vault where the Iceman lay. I followed him through the corridors of the anatomy building, an edifice that was as old and grave as a cathedral. Our voices echoing off the high ceilings, we passed somber murals depicting the dissection of the human body and then vast white-tiled rooms where the real thing was under way. Dozens of cadavers lay on tables while lab-coated medical students peeled back skin and cut away snippets of flesh. A fusty preservative smell penetrated every crevice of the building and the wrinkled brown bodies on the tables looked neither older nor younger, neither more nor less dead than that of the Neolithic man who had come out of the glacier.

It was into this bustling postmortem environment that the Iceman had been taken after his five millennia of perfect solitude. In the basement of the anatomy building, Platzer led me through a door marked *"Unbefugten ist der Zutritt verboten"* and into a large room with tile floors and several empty dissecting tables. Against one wall were two stout metal doors whose silvery surfaces had a pattern like crinkled aluminum foil.

Platzer opened the door on the right and showed me the dark, pantry-size chamber inside. "And so, behind the other door," he said, "is the body."

I stared at the rippled surface of the freezer door, wondering what sort of alarms would sound if I betrayed

Platzer's good faith and simply reached out, pulled the handle, and opened the vault. What brought me to the brink of this seditious conduct was the knowledge that the Iceman was just a few feet away from me, lying on his back in the subzero blackness that replicated his burial chamber in the glacier, his eyes staring at the ceiling, his stiff arm extended across his body. To his Stone Age family and friends, I suppose, he had lived on after his death as a wandering shade, since they had never been able to properly entomb his body and put his soul to rest. Was it *his* restless spirit I felt today in the basement of the anatomy building or merely my own, as I stood there imagining what was waiting to be revealed if I would only open that door?